The ENFIELD BOOK

This book is dedicated to the memory of Mrs Irene Smith, MBE (1932-1996), Secretary of Enfield Preservation Society, 1969-96, who died far too young

First published in 2007
by Historical Publications Ltd
32 Ellington Street, London N7 8PL
(Tel: 020 7607 1628)

ISBN 978-1-905286-20-1
British Library Cataloguing-in-Publication Data
A catalogue record for this book is available from the British Library

Reproduction by Tintern Graphics
Printed in Zaragoza, Spain by Edelvives

The Illustrations

All illustrations are reproduced by kind permission of the London Borough of Enfield except numbers 8, 11, 28, 50, 77, 91, 93, 165 which were supplied by the Publisher.

The ENFIELD BOOK

Graham Dalling

HISTORICAL PUBLICATIONS

Foreword

When writing *Enfield Past* (1999) a great deal of material had to be excluded for lack of space and much new research has been carried out since. When selecting material, I have worked on the well-tried principle that, if I find it interesting, so will my readers. If I have failed, I beg forgiveness.

There has inevitably been some repetition of material from *Enfield Past*, but I have tried to keep this to a minimum. When compiling biographical articles, I have deliberately excluded all references to living people. I have also omitted pubs from the book, as the subject has been dealt with so thoroughly by my friend, Gary Boudier, that there is little that I can usefully add.

I would like to thank my assistant, Kate Godfrey, for her help in preparing the typescript and the selection of illustrations. I would also like to acknowledge my debt to the work of former colleagues. David Pam, my line manager from 1973 until his retirement in 1982, has been a tower of strength and constant source of inspiration. Maureen Austin, my assistant for thirteen years prior to being made redundant in 1989, was loyal and hard working and with a refreshingly impish sense of humour. I also remain very much in debt to the work of my fellow local historians, in particular, Geoffrey Gillam, Steve Collins and the late Tom Lewis. Lastly, I must mention my friend, the late Frank Schofield, whose anarchic and frequently politically incorrect sense of humour helped to sustain me when all seemed lost.

I owe it to my employer to emphasise that the opinions expressed in this book are mine and mine alone.

Graham Dalling

Introduction

Enfield has since 1965 formed part of one of the largest London Boroughs. It is located on the extreme northern edge of the London conurbation and, with significant amounts of Green Belt land, large parts of Enfield have more in common with adjoining parts of Hertfordshire. It has not yet fully adjusted to being part of London and possibly never will.

Enfield was the largest of the ancient parishes in the old county of Middlesex and, lying in the north-east corner of the county, bordered directly on to both Essex and Hertfordshire. It formed part of the Edmonton Hundred together with South Mimms (including Potters Bar), Monken Hadley, Edmonton (including Southgate) and Tottenham (including Wood Green). Between 1837 and1930, for Poor Law purposes, Enfield was part of the Edmonton Union - the other parishes were Waltham Abbey, Cheshunt, Edmonton, Tottenham and Hornsey.

Enfield lay far enough from London not to be completely dominated by the metropolis and developed into a small market town rather than a large village. On the western side of the county Uxbridge, at more or less the same distance from London, developed on remarkably similar lines. When the author's grandfather was born in 1890, Enfield was not yet part of the London conurbation and there was still agricultural land separating it from Edmonton and Winchmore Hill to the south. It was only physically linked to London between the wars.

Communications (road, rail and river) run strongly north-south. The two major east-west roads, the North Circular and the M25 are both of recent origin and have made little impact on the outlook of Enfield people. The author, a native of Enfield, feels more or less at home in places as far away as Tottenham, Stoke Newington, Wood Green and Islington, while Barnet, Finchley, Walthamstow and Chingford, all closer to Enfield, but away from the north-south axis, have a distinctly foreign feel to them.

Enfield falls into two distinct halves. To the west lies Enfield Town, the traditional administrative and ecclesiastical centre. To the east, strung out along the Hertford Road lie the settlements of Ponders End, Enfield Highway, Enfield Wash and Freezywater, now merged into a solid conurbation firmly locked on to Edmonton in the south. Between the two halves lay the best arable land in the parish, which was not built over until recent times. The Great Cambridge Road (A10) was cut through this gap in the 1920s and now acts as a *cordon sanitaire* between the two halves of Enfield, which retain their essentially different characteristics. The author, growing up on the Willow Estate north of Enfield Town, knew Edmonton well and also visited Waltham Cross and Cheshunt (via Bullsmoor Lane), but most of East Enfield remained a no-go area, which he only got to know in more recent years.

Enfield is now irreversibly part of London, but the old Middlesex market town is not entirely dead and can be forgiven for the occasional wistful glance across the Hertfordshire border.

Text in bold type indicates a separate alphabetical entry.

John Abernethy

Abernethy (1764-1831) was Surgeon to St. Bartholomew's Hospital from 1815 to 1827. Although by no means the most skilful or innovative surgeon of his generation, he was a formidably good lecturer and a prolific writer of medical text books. He was also notoriously rude to his patients. In 1800 he married Ann Threlfall at All Saints Church, Edmonton, and the couple later acquired a house in Baker Street, Enfield (now demolished), which stood more or less opposite Rosemary Avenue on a site later occupied by a dairy. He died at Enfield

2. John Abernethy, surgeon to St Bartholomew's Hospital. There is a memorial to him in St Andrew's church.

and there is a memorial tablet to him in St. Andrew's Church.

Lt. Col. Reginald Applin

Conservative MP for Enfield (1924-9 and 1931-5), Applin (1869-1957) was educated at Sherborne, served in the British army 1889/1922, and was the author of a textbook on machine-gun tactics. He had hardline right-wing opinions, viewing the women's movement with misogynistic suspicion and vigorously opposing the proposal to lower the voting age for women from thirty to twenty-one. In the election of 1929 Applin lost his seat, when Enfield was retaken for Labour by **William Henderson** – the newly enfranchised women voters had taken their revenge. The election of 1931, held in a

1. Colonel Applin (left of the lady), MP for Enfield 1924-9 and 1931-5.

3. White Lodge, Silver Street, the home of Dr Jacob Asbury.

time of economic crisis immediately after the formation of the National Government, saw a collapse in the Labour vote and Applin regained Enfield for the Conservatives. He stood down in 1935, eventually settling in South Africa, where he must have found the regime rather more congenial.

Jacob Vale Asbury

Enfield's leading doctor in the first half of the 19th century, Jacob Asbury (1792-1871) lived at White Lodge, Silver Street and numbered **Charles Lamb** among his patients. In addition to his lucrative private practice Asbury was the Enfield parish surgeon and in 1837 he became medical officer to the Enfield Workhouse. In 1833 he published *A Treatise on Epidemic Cholera* in which he described treating no less than fifteen cases of the disease in Enfield. At the Workhouse he made great efforts to deal with skin diseases, especially scabies and ringworm, endemic among the parish children. Asbury supplied most of the public health data included in the General Board of Health Report on Enfield (1850).

Charles Babbage

Mathematician and inventor of calculating machines, Babbage (1792-1871) was educated in Enfield at the Rev. Stephen Freeman's Academy at Holmwood, a house formerly standing at the junction of Baker Street and Clay Hill. One of his fellow pupils was the future novelist **Frederick Marryat.** Most of his adult life was spent designing and building calculating machines, but despite spending large amounts of government money, his efforts were abortive, frustrated by the limitations of the technology of the time. In recent years a project at the Science Museum, using Babbage's drawings, has proved beyond doubt that the machines would have worked.

Baker Street

Baker Street is a continuation of Silver Street, with which it forms the principal link between Enfield Town and Forty Hill and Bulls Cross. It was known as Bakers Street in 1572. An alternative version, Beaker Street, appears only on the Rocque map of 1754.

Baptists

There was a Baptist presence in Enfield in the 17th century, but the cause did not take a firm hold until well into the 19th century. The original Enfield Baptist Church in London Road opened in 1875, moving in 1926 to a new building in Cecil Road. In East Enfield the

4. An early 20th-century view of Baker Street looking north towards Churchbury Road.

5. The first Enfield Baptist church (1875) in London Road, on a site occupied now by Woolworth's.

7. The present Enfield Baptist church in Cecil Road, dating from 1926.

8. Sir Joseph Bazalgette.

Totteridge Road Baptist Church opened in 1868 and the Suffolks Baptist Church opened in 1957, the fulfilment of a mission started in 1934.

Sir Joseph Bazalgette

The civil engineer, Joseph Bazalgette (1819-91) was born in Clay Hill, Enfield, the evidence from rate books suggesting at Hill Lodge, a large house formerly standing immediately east of The Fallow Buck. He trained under Sir John Macneill, who had been an assistant to Thomas Telford, and became a full member of the Institution of Civil Engineers in 1846. He was Chief Engineer to the Metropolitan Board of Works 1855-89, during which time he was responsible for building the London outfall sewers (1858-75), the Thames Embankment (1862-74), several Thames bridges (including Hammersmith) and some major road improvements including Charing Cross Road and Shaftesbury Avenue.

6. Hill Lodge, Clay Hill (demolished in 1965), the birthplace of Sir Joseph Bazalgette.

Beech Hill

One of the ancient trackways across Enfield Chase running west from Cockfosters Road to Monken Hadley and Barnet. The name derives from Beech Hill Park, whose northern boundary it forms. The western end retains the much older name of Camlet Way, derived from Camlet Moat, a medieval moated site on the northern edge of the Trent Park Estate. At the time of the 1851 census the section closest to the entrance to Hadley Common was known as Hadley Gate.

Adrian Bell

Bell (1901-80), was a prolific novelist, whose books were mostly set in rural East Anglia. His origins were anything but rural, being born in South London. During the First World War, unnerved by the Zeppelin raids, the Bell family moved to Enfield, settling in Uplands Park Road. In 1955 he wrote a novel entitled *A Young Man's Fancy*, the story of an adolescent boy growing up in London during that war. The book is partly set in Enfield and includes accurate descriptions of Enfield Town, Windmill Hill and The Ridgeway. Bell was also for many years a compiler of crosswords for the *The Times*. His son is the distinguished journalist and former Independent MP, Martin Bell.

Bell Lane

This was once a cart track leading to East Field and the marshland grazing areas beyond. The name derives from the nearby pub in the Hertford Road. The first houses had been built and occupied by the time of the 1871 census.

9. Election leaflet of 1983 for Sir Anthony Berry. He was killed a year later by the IRA bomb at Brighton.

Sir Anthony Berry

Berry (1925-1984) was the Conservative MP for Southgate (1964-74) and Enfield-Southgate (1974-84). He was the sixth son of Lord Kemsley, the press baron, and the nephew of another (Lord Camrose) and he had himself a distinguished career in journalism prior to entering Parliament. He held junior ministerial office in the Heath administration (1970/74) and was an opposition whip (1975-79). His life and career were brought to an abrupt and violent end by the IRA bomb at the Conservative Party Conference at Brighton in 1984. The bomber, Patrick Magee, was sentenced to eight life sentences, but under the terms of the Good Frday agreement, was released in 1999. Berry's daughter, Jo Tufnell, has aroused some controversy by meeting and discussing the bombing with Magee with a view to extracting something positive from the tragedy.

Sir John Betjeman

The most popular twentieth-century English poet and Poet Laureate from 1972 until his death, Betjeman (1906-84) was born at Kentish Town, later moving to Highgate. The family was of Dutch origin and owned a prosperous and long established cabinet-making business in Islington. Many of his poems include references to places in North London and

10. The cricket pitch at Heddon Court. In Betjeman's time, one of the masters in a drunken escapade drove his car across the pitch. The tyre marks were spotted and the culprit sacked.

the Middlesex suburbs such as Highbury Quadrant, Junction Road Station, Parliament Hill Fields, Aberdeen Park, Willesden and Harrow-on-the Hill. His verse autobiography, *Summoned by Bells*, includes descriptions of parts of Highgate, Kentish Town and Islington. After being sent down from Oxford, Betjeman was desperate for money and briefly took up teaching. From April 1929 to July 1930 he taught at the Heddon Court Preparatory School at Cockfosters. Many years later in his poem, *Cricket Master*, he recalled this time:

> *'What cared I for past disaster,*
> *Applicant for cricket master,*
> *Nothing much of cricket knowing,*
> *Conscious but of money owing.'*

The novelist Evelyn Waugh, a friend of Betjeman, visited him at Heddon Court. The house was a substantial property, standing in the angle between Cockfosters Road and Cat Hill. Soon after Betjeman's departure, it was sold and subsequently demolished, the name surviving in Heddon Court Avenue, one of the streets built on the estate.

Francis Augustus Bevan

Bevan (1840-1919) was born at Trent Park, the son of Robert Cooper Lee Bevan. The family was of Welsh origin, had originally been Quakers and had long been actively involved in Barclays Bank. (The Bank had originally traded as a partnership – Barclay, Bevan & Tritton.) When Barclays became a public company in 1896, Bevan became the first chairman, a post he held until his retirement in 1916. Locally, he served for many years as a churchwarden at Christ Church, Cockfosters, which had been built in 1839 largely at the expense of the Bevans. (The last of the family to maintain a link with Barclays Bank was Sir Timothy Bevan, Chairman 1981-87)

Sir John Bland Sutton

Bland-Sutton (1855-1936) was born at Green Street, Enfield Highway, one of the nine children of Charles William Sutton, a market gardener. He was educated at St James' School, later becoming a pupil teacher, and in 1878 he enrolled at the medical school at the Middlesex Hospital. In 1905 he became Surgeon to the Middlesex Hospital and in 1913 he founded and endowed the Institute of Pathology there.

Edward Blishen

Born and raised at Whetstone, Blishen (1920-1996) was a conscientious objector in World War II and subsequently trained as a teacher. He later became well known as a lecturer and broadcaster on education and children's literature. He was also a prolific writer, producing a series of gossipy, semi-fictionalised autobiographical books such as *Uncommon Entrance* (1974), *The Outside Contributor* (1986) and *Mind How You Go* (1997). Perhaps his best-known book is *A Cack-Handed War* (1972), set in the Second World War. He lived for many years until his death in Bartrams Lane, Hadley Wood. (In his books Hadley Wood appears, thinly disguised, as Barley Wood and Barnet as Barton.)

11. 'General' William Booth, founder of the Salvation Army.

William Booth

The founder of the Salvation Army was born and grew up in Nottingham. As a young man, Booth (1829-1912) became a lay preacher with the Methodist New Connection, but breaking with Methodism in 1861, he moved to London and four years later set up The Christian Mission at Whitechapel. In 1878 the name was changed to the more familiar Salvation Army with Booth as its first General. In 1889 he settled at Hadley Wood, initially living in Crescent East close to his son, Bramwell. In 1903 he moved to Rookstone (now no.33), Lancaster Avenue, a house built for him by the Salvation Army, where he lived until his death. He was succeeded as General by his son, Bramwell Booth, who held the post until being deposed shortly before his death in 1929. William, Bramwell and other family members were buried in a family plot at Abney Park Cemetery, Stoke Newington, where the graves can still be seen.

The settlement appears on Greenwoood's map of Middlesex (1829). The name is clearly an ironic allusion to the remoteness of the area and some rather exotic stories, concocted to link the place name with the transportation of prisoners to Australia, have no substance.

12. *The Elms (now Longbourn), Forty Hill, the childhood home of B J T Bosanquet.*

Bernard James Bosanquet

Bosanquet was a Middlesex and England cricketer, but more famously, inventor of the googly. Of Huguenot stock, Bosanquet (1877-1936) was born at Garnault, a substantial Victorian house still standing at Bulls Cross. The family later lived briefly at The Elms (now Longbourn), Forty Hill, before moving to the family home, **Clayesmore** in Clay Hill after the death of his grandfather, the wealthy banker James Whatman Bosanquet. (Bosanquet's Bank subsequently merged with Lloyds.) His son was the former ITN newsreader, Reginald Bosanquet, still fondly remembered for his alcohol fuelled gaffes in front of the cameras. There is a Bosanquet family tomb at Lavender Hill Cemetery.

Botany Bay

A small settlement on The Ridgeway between Enfield Town and Potters Bar which grew up after the enclosure of Enfield Chase in 1777 close to **East Lodge**, one of the former hunting lodges on the Chase.

Edward Augustus 'Gussie' Bowles

The younger son of H C B Bowles of Myddelton House and the brother of **Sir Henry Bowles**, Edward Bowles (1865-1954) became a formidably gifted gardener, creating a world famous garden at Myddelton House. He was a prolific author of books on gardening and related topics, including the justly acclaimed *My garden in Spring* (1914), *My garden in Summer* (1914) and *My garden in Autumn & Winter* (1915). He was elected to the Council of the Royal Horticultural Society in 1908. Locally he founded a night school at Turkey Street, and the Forty Hill Mutual Improvement Horticul-

13. *Edward August 'Gussie' Bowles, pictured in his garden at Myddelton House.*

14. Sir Henry Bowles.

tural Society and he also ran an unofficial club for boys at Myddelton House. He also served for many years as a lay reader at Jesus Church, Forty Hill.

Sir Henry Bowles

Sir Henry (1858-1943) was Conservative MP for Enfield (1889-1906 and 1918-23), and was the only Enfield MP to have been born locally. He was a son of H C B Bowles of Myddelton House and the elder brother of **E.A. 'Gussie' Bowles**, the eminent horticulturalist. Sir Henry lived at Forty Hall, which his father bought for him as a present. His mother, Cornelia Kingdom, was related to Sophia Kingdom, who married the French-born engineer, Marc Brunel, the father of Isambard.

Suffering from a crippling stammer, Bowles was no great orator, but nonetheless was apparently popular in the constituency. It has also been suggested that his many tenants and estate workers, some out of genuine loyalty and others not trusting the secrecy of the ballot, were among his strongest supporters. He took great interest in the workers at the Royal Small Arms Factory at Enfield Lock. Nevertheless, he was decisively defeated by a Liberal, James Branch, in the election of 1906, but in 1918 the Enfield Conservatives, short of a candidate when John Pretyman Newman defected to Finchley, invited Bowles, by now aged sixty, to stand again for Enfield. He was successfully elected and held Enfield until standing down in 1922.

Outwardly a pillar of respectable society, Bowles' private life was not all that it might have been. The travel writer, **Norman Lewis** (also born in Enfield), in *Jackdaw Cake* and *God Bless the Squire* exposed Bowles' marital infidelities with mischievous glee. Luckily for Bowles, the tabloid press of his time knew better than to interfere with the pleasures of the rich and powerful.

James Branch

James Branch (1845-1918) was Liberal MP for Enfield (1906-10), winning the seat in the great Liberal landslide, and unseating the Conservative, **Captain** (later **Sir Henry**) **Bowles**) Branch was a boot manufacturer, who gained his political experience as a Progressive councillor on the London County Council. A staunch nonconformist, when the election result was declared, he immediately fell to his knees to pray and give thanks. He took up the cause of the people of Palmers Green and Winchmore Hill (then in his constituency) who had been suffering from a spate of burglaries and other crimes. The result of this was a new police station at Winchmore Hill. He raised the issue of the Great Eastern Railway's withdrawal of the passenger service on the Southbury Loop in 1909. On this occasion his intervention was unsuccessful and the line remained closed. In the election of January 1910 the Enfield electorate had a change of heart and rejected Branch in favour of a Conservative again, J R Pretyman Newman - Branch did not feel the need to give thanks on this occasion.

Brick Lane

This road appears on the Enclosure Map of 1803, but was apparently unnamed at this time. The name first appears on the Ordnance Survey map of 1867 and is a reminder of the brick making industry once so prominent in East Enfield.

Brigadier Hill

The name was in use by 1850 and was sometimes applied to parts of Phipps Hatch Lane and Cocker Lane (Browning Road). A Brigadier House formerly stood on the site of St Luke's Church at the junction of Phipps Hatch Lane and Browning Road - the name was later appropriated by another house still standing at the foot of Brigadier Hill.

Brimsdown

This is a heavily industrialised district on the eastern edge of Enfield, north of Ponders End. It incorporates the ancient hamlet of Green Street of which the principal survivals are two pubs - the Golden Hive and the White Horse - and a pair of timber framed houses (nos.98-100), originally a single property. Brimsdown Station on the Great Eastern's Lea Valley Line opened in 1884. In 1904 the North Metropolitan Electric Power Supply Co. opened Brimsdown Power Station on

15. The foot of Brigadier Hill in 1974. Parts of this road remained remarkably rural until the late 1960s.

16. An early 20th-century view of Green Street showing the White Horse and the Golden Hive.

a site between the railway and the Lee Navigation. The availability of cheap electricity encouraged industrial development and by 1939 a huge complex of factories had grown up to the east of the railway, many having their own sidings.

Browning Road

The road was originally called Cocker Lane – it appears thus on the 1754 Tithe Map and the Chase Enclosure Map of 1777. The name of Browning Road was in use by 1892 and was derived not from the poet, but from a Browning family formerly resident at Brigadier House (on the site of St. Luke's Church and not the present Brigadier House at the foot of Brigadier Hill).

Bartle Bull

Bartle Bull (1902-1950) was Conservative MP for Enfield from 1935 to 1945. He was a barrister by profession. Bull held junior ministerial posts at the Treasury, the Ministry of Transport and the Ministry of Fuel and Power, but his career was cut short by the landslide Labour victory in the 1945 election in which his seat was decisively taken by **Ernest Davies** for the Labour Party. At the time of his death he was engaged in legal action for defamation against a person who had accused him of drunkenness.

17. An extension to Brimsdown Power Station under construction in 1939.

Bulls Cross

This road runs due north from Maidens Bridge and Forty Hill to the Hertfordshire boundary. It follows the alignment of Roman **Ermine Street** which can be followed further north through the Theobalds Estate. It was known as Bulls Cross Lane in 1572, the name probably deriving from a former wayside cross.

Buses and Coaches

Before the railway era passenger traffic to and from Enfield was largely in the hands of short-stage coaches, which took advantage of the improved turnpike roads. From the 1830s these vehicles were gradually replaced by larger-bodied horse omnibuses with greater carrying capacity. In 1790 James Dickenson was making five re-

18. A late 19th-century view of the Pied Bull, Bulls Cross.

19. Maidens Bridge (over Turkey Brook) linking Bulls Cross to Forty Hill.

turn journeys daily between Enfield Town and the City, calling at The Bull, Bishopsgate and The Castle and Falcon, Aldersgate.

Enfield was also served by long-distance stage coaches using the Hertford Road. In 1826 coaches were passing through Enfield on their way to Boston, Cambridge, Edinburgh, Fakenham, King's Lynn, Stamford, Wisbech and York. By travelling via Enfield, Royston and Huntingdon, they avoided Barnet Hill and Highgate Hill on the Great North Road and had a quicker and easier exit from the capital.

By 1826 John Glover was operating a regular coach service between Enfield Town and the Flower Pot, Bishopsgate at a fare of 2/6d return. He was later joined in the business by his younger brothers, Newman, who lived at Uvedale Cottage, Holly Walk, and William, who was also landlord of the King's Head. (For those who were prepared to walk to Edmonton there was a more frequent service and cheaper fares.) By 1845 the Glovers were making seven re-

20. A pirate bus operated by Redburn's.

21. A group of Redburn's staff, probably taken at the depot at Green Street.

turn journeys daily to the City.

The first railway in Enfield was the Lea Valley Line (1840) but it was located too far east to make any impact on the horse buses serving Enfield Town. However, when the branch line to Enfield Town came in 1849, despite its high fares and a circuitous route via Angel Road and Stratford, it put the Glovers out of business by 1855. In 1865 Charles Case briefly attempted two round trips daily between the King's Head and Westminster Abbey via Green Lanes.

The opening of the Great Northern Railway's Enfield Branch (1871) and the Great Eastern Railway's direct line to Enfield (1872) effectively killed off horse buses on the longer distance routes. They survived by providing feeder services from outlying districts such as Forty Hill to the main railway stations.

With the invention of the internal combustion engine the bus was revitalised. In 1906 Ensign Buses provided a short-lived service between Edmonton and Waltham Cross. The mighty London General Omnibus Co. finally extended its activities into Enfield in 1913 when the 29 route from Victoria, which had reached Southgate in 1912, was extended to Cockfosters. (The company opened a bus garage at Palmers Green in a converted roller skating rink in 1912.)

During the First World War many servicemen acquired experience of motor vehicles and, after being demobbed, moved into the fields of road haulage and buses. The new small bus companies, nicknamed 'pirates', found themselves in competition with the established services of London General, and in north London the 29 route saw some particularly ferocious competition.

There were several pirate companies either based in Enfield or operating local services. One of the largest was Admiral, based at Willow Walk (near Turnpike Lane). The owner, A T Bennett, lived at Green Dragon Lane, Winchmore Hill, later moving to Adelaide House, Forty Hill. Admiral operated many services including the 280 route, which linked Forty Hill with Finsbury Park. Another substantial company was Redburn Motor Services, who operated from a garage at Green Street, Enfield Highway, The Prince Omnibus Co. was based in South Street, Ponders End. Some of the companies were very small, such as GWL, run by the Lewington brothers as an adjunct to their bicycle shop in Enfield Wash, and the Perkins family, which operated buses from a small yard adjoining their home in Lancaster Road.

London General responded by buying up the competition. In this, A T Bennett of Admiral played a decidedly ambiguous role. He established the London Public Omnibus Co. in 1927, ostensibly as a confederation of small bus operators, but in reality cover for London General's efforts to buy out the pirates. London General built a bus garage in Southbury Road, Ponders End in 1927, but then leased it almost immediately to London Public. The pirate era ended in 1933, when all bus services in Greater London and the surrounding area were brought under the control of the London Passenger Transport Board, the direct ancestor of Transport for London. (As the new organisation was dominated by former LGOC staff, London General had effectively won.)

By 1938 many routes that still function today were already running. The 204 from Lower Edmonton Station to Gordon Hill was later extended to Chase Farm Hospital and renumbered 128. (In 1968 it was again renumbered W8 and was the first bus route in Enfield to go over to one man operation.) The 144, 144A and 144B had all started as offshoots of the 29 route. The

144A from Muswell Hill to the Halfway House became the 217 and 144B from Muswell Hill to Forty Hill became the 231. The 107 (Arkley to Ponders End) and 107A (Ponders End to the Royal Small Arms Factory) were the direct ancestors of the 307. Green Line was operating the M1 from Hertford to Guildford via Enfield – revived after the last war as the 715, it was for many years a useful link between Enfield and the West End. The Country Bus operation included the 310 (Enfield to Hertford) and the 313 (Enfield to St Albans via Potters Bar).

Since the last war the number of bus passengers has declined, a process that started with the abolition of petrol rationing and the continued growth of car ownership; it has only been partially reversed by such measures as free travel passes for pensioners.

Changes to the network have included the absorption of the former trolleybus routes when they were converted to conventional diesel buses in 1961. (Many of the route numbers, such as the 279, still include elements of the old tram numbers.) In 1968 there was a major reorganisation centred on Turnpike Lane, which became the main hub and interchange point for much of North London's bus routes. It is too early to assess the effect of more recent changes such as partial privatisation and the introduction of Oyster cards. (The shareholders of Arriva, Stage Coach and First Group have undoubtedly benefited from the large influx of public money, but whether passengers will remains to be seen.)

Bullsmoor Lane

Bullsmoor Lane runs due east from **Bulls Cross** and the A10 to the Hertford Road and is now one of the most heavily used roads in Enfield, carrying traffic to and from the M25. In 1754 it was called Belsmoor Lane. The Great Eastern Railway's Southbury Loop of 1891 was originally intended to cross Bullsmoor Lane by means of a level crossing, but pressure from the local authority forced the railway company to build a bridge.

Bush Hill Park

This modern, residential suburb straddling the former Edmonton/Enfield border, conceals the remains of the earliest known settlement in the district. Extensive Roman remains have come to light especially between 1974 and 1976, when excavations took place between Lincoln Road and Main Avenue on land cleared for redevelopment. The settlement here appears to have been abandoned at the end of the Roman occupation and the area saw little human habitation until it began to develop in the late 19th century.

The Edmonton enclosure map (1801) and the Enfield enclosure map (1803) both show Bush Hill Park as almost entirely undeveloped. There were no houses along the entire length of Lincoln Road, and along the southern fringe was just the remote hamlet of Bury Street. At this time the bulk of the land between Bury Street and Lincoln Road was owned by **William Mellish**, who lived at a large house called Bush Hill Park, that stood on the slopes of Bush Hill on a site now occupied by Ringmer Place.

After Mellish's death, and several changes of ownership, the estate was sold in 1871 and broken up for building. Development accelerated after 1880 when the Great Eastern Railway opened Bush Hill Park station on its existing line.

The first houses in Wellington Road and Village Road went on the market in 1878. The first inhabitants were solidly middle class, attracted by the large detached houses and the spacious, tree-lined roads.

To the east of the railway development took place on very different lines. Plans were submitted for The Avenues in 1880, and the Cardigan Estate was developed in two phases in 1889 and 1892. The area was

22. Bush Hill Park in its heyday – a leafy scene in Wellington Road.

developed with small terraced houses and the newcomers were predominantly working class, including many railway employees: drivers, firemen and guards based at Enfield Town depot.

A Church of England school, St Mark's in Main Avenue, was opened by 1882 (the building survives as the Bush Hill Park Library). This proved to be totally inadequate and the resulting shortfall in school places was one of the key factors that led to the Board of Education ordering the establishment of the Enfield School Board in 1894. The Board opened Bush Hill Park School in Main Avenue in 1896. (The Edmonton part of Bush Hill Park had to wait until 1928 when a school was built in Raglan Road.)

The new suburb was initially without any place of worship. The Church of England built St Mark's Church in 1893, followed by St Stephen's in 1907. A Congregational church (now United Reformed) was opened in Main Avenue and a Primitive Methodist church was built in 1905 in Wellington Road.

Development continued uninterrupted until the First World War. In 1909 a tramway was initiated along Village Road and Park Avenue – a route chosen because trams could not manage the gradients on the old main road over Bush Hill. By 1914 Bush Hill Park (east of the railway) was more or less fully developed. On the west side the area to the north of Park Avenue was fully built up and building had begun to the south (Edenbridge Road, Bagshot Road etc.). This was resumed after the war with the development of the New River Estate; the first houses in Sittingbourne Avenue and Faversham Avenue were occupied by 1926. By 1935 Bush Hill Park was fully developed. Further improvement in transport facilities came with the construction of the Great Cambridge Road which was largely complete by 1924.

After the last war the gaps caused by bombing were filled. (One of the largest was caused by a V2 rocket which fell in Abbey Road.) The Village Road/Wellington Road area saw a process of gradual redevelopment: large detached houses were demolished one by one, giving way to blocks of flats. To the east of the railway, change was much more drastic. A large area between Main Avenue and Lincoln Road was compulsorily purchased and redeveloped with not entirely satisfactory results, but the scheme did at least allow archaeologists to investigate the site.

Today, the two halves of Bush Hill Park retain their different characteristics and the communities remain largely self-contained, the only shared facility being the railway station. Bush Hill Park, the house on Bush Hill which gave its name to the suburb, was demolished in 1927, but one of its

23. John By's works at the Royal Small Arms Factory, viewed across floodwater in December 1914.

neighbours has been more fortunate. **Old Park** survives as the Bush Hill Park Golf Club. Bush Hill House (Halliwick), shorn of most of its grounds and drastically altered survived as a residential school for disabled children until 1993, when it was peremptorily demolished to make way for yet more flats.

John By

Born in Lambeth, By (1779-1836) had a successful army career in the Royal Engineers, rising to the rank of Lieutenant Colonel. In 1814, with help from John Rennie, By prepared the plans for the Royal Small Arms Factory at Enfield Lock, some remnants of which survive in the otherwise undistinguished Enfield Island Village. In 1826 he was recalled for service in Canada, where he supervised the construction of the Ottawa Canal and the Rideau Canal. He founded the small settlement of Bytown, which now forms the core of the Canadian capital, Ottawa. He retired to England, settling in the Sussex village of Frant, where his memorial survives in the church.

Elizabeth Canning

Elizabeth Canning, aged eighteen, achieved both celebrity and notoriety in 1754. She disappeared on New Year's Day while on her way home from visiting her aunt and uncle and four weeks later she turned up at her mother's home at Aldermanbury in the City in a dishevelled and emaciated state. She claimed that she had been attacked by two men at Houndsditch, who had robbed her and dragged her several miles to a house where she had been imprisoned in an upstairs room and efforts made to lure her into prostitution. Eventually she escaped by pulling loose a board covering a window and jumping down to ground level and eventually found her way home.

24. Elizabeth Canning on trial for perjury.

25. Elizabeth Canning, allegedly kidnapped and held against her will at Enfield Wash in 1754.

Based on her evidence the house was identified as the home of Mother Wells, a house of ill repute, once a pub, standing in Hertford Road, Enfield Wash at the junction with Ordnance Road. A search party was sent out, resulting in the arrest of Susannah Wells, Virtue Hall and Mary Squires, who were promptly tried and convicted. Serious doubts then arose about the evidence, the accused were pardoned, and Elizabeth Canning was tried for perjury, convicted, and transported to the American colonies. The case was hugely controversial at the time and has remained so. One could easily fill a bookcase with the literature generated by the Canning case over a period of 250 years.

Capel House

This large 18th-century house stands on the north side of Bullsmoor Lane. It was built for Rawson Hart Boddam, a former East India Company official who had risen to be Governor of Bombay. It was later the home

26. Capel House, now a horticultural college, built for a former Governor of Bombay.

28. John Cartwright.

of the Warren family, wealthy tea merchants. It is now occupied by the Capel Manor Horticultural College.

Richard Carlile

Carlile (1790-1843), born in Devon, was a printer, political agitator, atheist and journalist. By publishing the works of Thomas Paine and editing the radical journal, *The Republican*, he incurred the wrath of the repressive government of the day. In particular the authorities were angry at his first hand reporting of the Peterloo Massacre in Manchester in 1819. Carlile served several terms of imprisonment - his wife, who published during his absence, was also jailed. In 1830 he was imprisoned again for seditious libel for writing an article in support of agricultural labourers campaigning against wage cuts. His monument in later years was a free press. Between 1835 and 1842, he lived in some poverty at Enfield Highway. He was buried at Kensal Green Cemetery.

Carterhatch Lane

This road runs due east from Forty Hill to the Hertford Road and is now intersected by the A10. It was known as Carter Hatch Lane as early as 1572, the name possibly deriving from a former gate (an old word for gate being hatch), but the site is too far east for it to have been a gate onto Enfield Chase. Alternative names have included Cartwright's Lane, Syms Lane and Potash Lane.

John Cartwright

Cartwright (1740-1824) is often known as the 'Father of Reform', and is commemorated for his radical political life, which included campaigns for manhood suffrage and the end of slavery, in Cartwright Gardens near St Pancras Station where he resided from 1820 until his death.

He lived in Enfield at a house in Chase Hill (off Chase Green) for some years around 1805.

27. Carterhatch Lane in 1912, still looking remarkably rural.

Among his friends at this time was **Charles Cowden Clarke**. Cartwright was buried at Finchley, where his monument can still be seen in St Mary's churchyard.

Cat Hill

Mostly in East Barnet, this road follows the line of an ancient trackway from the Bohun or Bourn Gate of Enfield Chase (on the site of the Cockfosters roundabout) towards Barnet. The name came from a pub that stood at the foot of the hill.

Cattlegate Road

This runs along the northern edge of the former Enfield Chase from Theobalds Park Road towards Northaw. The name of the road derives from a former gate to the Chase that stood at the junction with Cooper's Lane Road, but that was named after Cathale Priory, an obscure and short-lived religious foundation on the border between Enfield and Northaw.

Cemeteries

Until 1872 Enfield's principal burial ground was St Andrew's churchyard in Enfield Town, but even early in that century it was fast approaching saturation point and in 1846 a large extension was opened to the north of Holly Walk. Despite this, by the 1860s the health hazard was obvious and pupils at the nearby Enfield Grammar School had to endure an all-pervading smell from the burial ground.

St James, Enfield Highway (1831) and Christ Church, Cockfosters (1839) both had churchyards. Of the nonconformist churches, the former Zion Chapel in Chase Side (on the site of Christ Church URC) had a burial ground from which a few gravestones survive. (In 2004 the construction of an invalid ramp at the adjoining church hall inadvertently resulted in the disturbance of human remains.)

In 1870 the Enfield Burial Board was set up, and a large plot of land at Lavender Hill was acquired, laid out as a cemetery and opened in 1872. Two chapels were provided, one for the Church of England

29. Overcrowded conditions at St Andrew's churchyard became a health hazard and resulted in the opening of Lavender Hill Cemetery.

30. Lavender Hill Cemetery, opened in 1872.

and one for the nonconformists. Another cemetery was later built at Enfield Highway on a site adjoining St James' churchyard. In 1920 the Burial Board was wound up and its functions taken over by Enfield Urban District Council. Today, both cemeteries remain in use, but only Lavender Hill now has much room for expansion.

The Adath Yisrael Cemetery (Jewish) in Carterhatch Lane opened in 1924. Another Jewish cemetery has been established on the northern edge of Enfield at Bulls Cross Ride by the Western Synagogue, whose previous cemetery at Montagu Road, Edmonton (opened in 1884) was full.

31. A delightful early 20th-century view of Chalk Lane, Cockfosters, showing the spire of Christ Church (1839) and the pond (now filled in).

Chalk Lane

This turning on the west side of Cockfosters Road leads to Monken Hadley Common. The name is obscure in origin as the subsoil consists of clay and gravel and not chalk. It may be significant that at Chalk Farm in Camden, the name derives from *'chaldecote'*, meaning a shelter for travellers in cold weather.

Chapel Street

Formerly called Love's Row, this was an exceptionally unhealthy street suffering from overcrowding, bad drainage and contaminated drinking water. There was a cholera outbreak here in 1866. The old cottages were bombed in the last war and later replaced by a rather bland block of council flats.

32. Chase Side looking north towards Christ Church. The muddy track to the left is now Chase Green Avenue.

33. Chase Side looking north towards Halifax Road and Gordon Road. The shop at the corner of Halifax Road is still an off-licence.

34. The stables at Chase Side House awaiting demolition in 1901.

Chase Side

So-called because it ran along the eastern boundary of Enfield Chase - Chase Side, Southgate ran along the western boundary. The northern end was known as Holly Bush from the pub of that name that still stands at the junction with Lancaster Road. In 1572, the road was known as Little Woodside.

Chase Side House

A substantial property, probably of early 19th-century date, this house stood on the western edge of Enfield Town on the site of the Library Green. It was for many years the home of Philip Twells, Conservative MP for the City of London and a director of Barclay's Bank. His widow endowed St. Mary Magdalene's church on Windmill Hill in his memory. After her death the house was de-

35. Chase Side House in 1873. It stood on the site of the Library Green and was demolished in 1901.

36. Church Lane in 1955. The cottages were demolished for an inner ring road scheme that never materialised.

37. Jesus Church, Forty Hill, was built in 1835 by Thomas Ashwell. It is a copy of James Savage's Holy Trinity at Tottenham Green.

molished and the estate broken up, a substantial portion being purchased by Enfield Council in 1901 to form the Town Park. Remains of the foundations and filled-in cellars survive beneath the Library Green and were accidentally rediscovered during the digging of ARP trenches during the last war.

Church Lane

This road appears on the Enclosure Map of 1803. The name, in use by the time of the 1841 census, derives from the nearby St Andrew's church and vicarage. A scheme for an inner ring road at Enfield Town (rejected by central government in 1967) would have obliterated Church Lane, but sadly a perfectly sound row of early 19th-century cottages had already been demolished in anticipation of the scheme – the site is currently a rather cramped car park.

Church of England churches

Until the early 19th century **St Andrew's Church** in Enfield Town, a substantial medieval building, was sufficient for Enfield's spiritual needs.

Population growth made the provision of new churches a necessity. St James', Enfield Highway (1831) was followed in quick succession by Jesus Church, Forty Hill (1835) and Christ Church, Cockfosters (1839). St John's, Clay Hill (1857) was built and paid for by the **Rev. John Moore Heath,** the then vicar of St Andrew's. This was followed by St Michael and All Angels, Gordon Hill (1874), St Matthew's Ponders End (1878), St Mary Magdalene, Windmill Hill (1883), St Mark's, Bush Hill Park

38. *St John's, Clay Hill, built to the designs of J P St Aubyn.*

39. *An early 20th-century view of Church Street looking west. The wall to the right belongs to Burleigh House (demolished 1913).*

(1892), St. Luke's, Browning Road (1900), and St George's, Freezywater (1906). St Paul's Hadley Wood was built in 1911 - despite being well supported and well financed, it is still technically a chapel of ease to Christ Church, Cockfosters. After the First World War the impetus slowed. St Peter and St Paul, Ordnance Road was

40. *Churchbury House in Churchbury Lane (p26), then largely rural. The house is now converted into two flats and is surrounded by modern housing.*

built in 1928, replacing the former Royal Small Arms Factory Chapel. (This was wrecked in 1944 by the same V1 that damaged Chesterfield Road School – a new church was built in 1969.) St Peter's, Grange Park was under construction when the last war broke out and was consecrated in 1941. St. Giles, Bullsmoor Lane opened in 1954 as a chapel of ease to Jesus Church. Early promise was ultimately not fulfilled and the church closed and was subsequently destroyed by fire.

42. The Queen's Hall Cinema, newly rebuilt in 1928. Re-opened in 1947 after bomb damage, it was renamed The Florida. Later used as a night club, it was demolished for an extension of Genotin Road.

Church Street

The principal shopping street of Enfield Town, the name of which reflects the proximity of St Andrew's church. In old records it was sometimes included as part of The Town and sometimes referred to as High Street.

Churchbury Lane

This road was made up from an old field track after enclosure (1803), the name deriving from the former Churchbury Field along whose eastern boundary it ran. It was also known as Cherry Orchard

41. The Ponders End Electric Theatre, opened in 1913 and closed in 1940 after bomb damage. The building is now a pub.

Lane from the orchards that once lined the road – many of the fruit trees still survive in the gardens.

Cinemas

Enfield's first cinema, the Enfield Empire, used a converted hall in Silver Street in 1909 and survived until 1917. In 1911 The Picturedrome opened in a former brewery in Horseshoe Lane, but had closed by the end of the First World War, the building surviving for many years as a pharmaceutical warehouse.

The first purpose-built cinema, the Queen's Hall in London Road, opened in 1911. This was rebuilt for sound in 1928, bomb-damaged in 1940, re-opened in 1947 as The Florida, closed in 1976, converted into a night club (The Town House), and finally was closed and demolished to make way for an extension of Genotin Road.

The Ponders End Electric Theatre opened in 1913, but closed after bomb damage in 1940. It was converted by Enfield Council into a public hall, and then later sold off and re-emerged as a pub. The Rialto in Burleigh Way opened 1920, was re-named Granada in 1967, closed in 1971, re-opened as a bingo hall and closed yet again – the building, currently empty, is being greedily eyed by property developers.

The Premier in Hertford Road, opened in 1921, was wired for sound in 1930, closed in 1961, and then used as a bingo hall until final closure and demolition in 1985. The Savoy in Southbury Road opened in 1935, was later an ABC and eventually the Canon. Despite being subdivided to provide a multi-screen facility, much of the original décor survived. Although still well supported, it closed suddenly in 1997 and was quickly demolished to make way for a Tesco supermarket.

43. Charles Cowden Clarke's home in Nag's Head Lane (Southbury Road), where his father, John Clarke, ran a private school. It was later incorporated into Enfield Town Station and demolished in 1872.

Cineworld, incorporated in a new leisure development in Southbury Road, is now the only working cinema in Enfield.

Charles Cowden Clarke

The Shakespearean scholar, Charles Cowden Clarke (1787-1877), grew up in Enfield Town, where his father, John Clarke, ran a boys' boarding school in Nag's Head Lane (now Southbury Road) on the site of Enfield Town Station. His maternal grandfather was Rev. John Ryland, a distinguished nonconformist clergyman. One of his father's pupils was the young John Keats, who became a close friend. His wife, Mary, came from a distinguished musical family, the Novellos, of Italian extraction. Her father, Vincent Novello, was the founder of the famous music publishing firm that still bears his name, and her sister, Clara, was an accomplished singer. *Recollections of Writers*, jointly written by Charles and Mary, contains useful material on Keats and Charles Lamb, whom he also knew, and interesting references to Enfield.

44. Clay Hill in the early 20th century, showing the Rose and Crown.

45. The lodge at Clayesmore, once the home of the Bosanquet family.

Charles and Mary were also the joint authors of a once popular concordance to Shakespeare. Mary's autobiography, *My Long Life*, also contains Enfield references, including recollections of her honeymoon spent at the former Greyhound Inn in Enfield Town.

Clay Hill

The name was in use by 1572 and probably derives from a former landowner rather than soil conditions. The settlement adjoining the Rose and Crown was also known as Bridge Street, the name still appearing in legal documents into the early 19th century.

Clayesmore

This was a substantial property standing on the north side of Clay Hill. It was owned in the early 19th century by Mrs Ann Hume, and was later acquired by Edward Harman, on whose bankruptcy, in 1847, it was purchased by James Whatman Bosanquet. The house was briefly occupied in the early 20th century by Alex Devine, who ran a boys' preparatory school. (This moved to Pangbourne, Berkshire and then to Iwerne Minster, Dorset, where it still survives and still uses the name Clayesmore.) The house was demolished in the late thirties, but a small lodge house has survived.

Cockfosters and Hadley Wood

These settlements grew up on what had been the north-west corner of **Enfield Chase**, a former royal hunting ground, after it was enclosed in 1777. In its natural state it was covered by a mixture of scrub and forest as can still be seen on Hadley Common and parts of Trent Park. There were three lodges on the Chase, one of which was **West Lodge** (on the site of the present West Lodge Hotel). This corner of the Chase figured in national history in 1471, when the so-called Battle of Barnet was fought in and around Monken Hadley village, an overwhelming victory for the Yorkist army of King Edward IV. His opponent, Warwick the Kingmaker, died on the battlefield.

The enclosure of the Chase saw the creation of two new estates. Francis Russell, the surveyor responsible for the enclosure, acquired 152 acres of land on which he built himself a mansion: Beech Hill Park.

46. An early 20th-century view of Trent Park showing the house as it was during the Bevan era.

47. Trent Park as transformed by Sir Philip Sassoon. The bricks came from Devonshire House, Piccadilly.

Elsewhere on the Chase, Richard Jebb, a popular society doctor, was granted a lease on three adjoining plots of former Chase land. He built a house which he named Trent Place, after Trento in the Tyrol where in 1777 Jebb had cured the Duke of Gloucester, brother of King George III, of a serious illness. This house was progressively enlarged by successive owners and came to be known as Trent Park.

By 1867 a small settlement, virtually an estate village for Trent Park, had grown up at Cockfosters. Its main component was a collection of cottages on the west side of Cockfosters Road (north of the main gate to Trent Park). There was a collection of larger houses and a pub (The Cock) in **Chalk Lane**. Also in Chalk Lane was Christ Church, built in 1839 and paid for by Robert Cooper Lee Bevan of Trent Park. (The **Bevans**, who were partners in Barclays Bank, held Trent Park from 1833 to 1908). To the south of Chalk Lane, a row of cottages (Woodside Cottages) lay on the east side of Cockfosters Road at right angles to the road. In the angle between Cockfosters Road and Cat Hill stood Belmont, a substantial house in its own grounds, later known as Heddon Court.

At Hadley Wood, development was at an even more primitive level. There were three large houses (West Lodge, Beech Hill Park and Greenwood) plus two small groups of cottages sited on the north side of Camlet Way. There had been no development at all in Wagon Road. The Great Northern Railway's main line had been opened in 1850, the construction involving the boring of two major tunnels. However, at first no station was provided for Hadley Wood.

In the early 1880s Charles Jack, the owner of Beech Hill Park, drew up plans to develop much of Hadley Wood, and in 1882 he signed a building lease with the Duchy of Lancaster to lay out streets. Negotiations with the Great Northern Railway resulted in the opening of a station at Hadley Wood in 1885 and by 1896 Crescent Road (later Crescent East and Crescent West) was partly built up. Some large detached houses appeared on the North side of Beech Hill. Lancaster Avenue was laid out, but as yet was without houses. By 1914, apart from the addition of a few houses in Lancaster Avenue, Hadley Wood had barely grown.

Cockfosters hardly altered at all during the late 19th century: the 1914 Ordnance Survey maps differ only marginally from those of 1867. Two of the larger houses, Heddon Court (Belmont) and Ludgrove, had become boys' preparatory schools.

Trent Park was sold in 1908 to Sir Edward Sassoon and on his death in 1912 the house passed to his son **Sir Philip Sassoon** After an abortive attempt to break up the estate for building, the Beech Hill Park estate was converted into a golf course in 1922, the mansion becoming the club house.

The Piccadilly Line reached Cockfosters in July 1933 and the great building boom which had overwhelmed Southgate spilled across the border. Heddon Court and Westpole Farm were sold for building and streets were laid out, and by 1939 Cockfosters, as far north as the station, was part of suburban London. However, development of the housing estates was by no means complete and there were many gaps which were filled in the early 1950s. The introduction of the Green Belt prevented any further expansion northwards and the London conurbation still ends somewhat abruptly by the junction of Cockfosters Road and Chalk Lane. North of this point the east side of Cockfosters Road remains farmland, while on the west side, thin ribbon development links Cockfosters to Hadley Wood.

Sir Philip Sassoon died in the summer of 1939 and during the last war his house, Trent Park, became an interrogation centre for high-ranking German prisoners of war. The house subsequently became a teacher training college, merging into the Middlesex Polytechnic (now university) in 1974. The estate was purchased by the former Middlesex County Council and was opened to the public in 1973 by the Greater London Council.

48. Cooper's Lane Road c.1890, with a passing farm cart.

Since the last war the gaps left on the pre-war estates at Cockfosters have been filled. At Hadley Wood some further limited housing development took place. Hadley Wood station was rebuilt in 1959 as part of a scheme for widening the line at this point, the work being on a large scale and involving the boring of extra tunnels. The line was electrified in 1976.

The last war and the introduction of the Green Belt have left Cockfosters and Hadley Wood in a half and half state. They are now a slightly odd mixture of open country and opulent outer suburbia.

Cockfosters Road

This is part of an ancient trackway across Enfield Chase linking Southgate with Potters Bar. The southern section is known as Chase Side (Southgate), the northern continuation is called Stagg Hill (from a former pub) and the section within Potters Bar is called Southgate Road.

Co-operative Movement

The Enfield Highway Co-operative Society was founded in 1872 by a group of workers at the Royal Small Arms Factory, following the example set by the Woolwich Arsenal Co-op. (The Enfield Town society, which began after the Enfield Highway Co-op, was short-lived, having run into financial trouble and had to be rescued.) Business expanded and eventually the Enfield Highway Co-op served a much larger area with shops as far away as Hertford and Waltham Abbey. A proposed merger with the Luton Co-op failed to materialise, but the Society later joined with the St Albans Co-op to form the Enfield and St Albans Co-operative Society. In recent years, shying away from direct competition with the big supermarkets, it has moved increasingly into the convenience store sector of the market.

Cooper's Lane Road

Shown on the Enfield Chase Enclosure Map of 1777, Cooper's Lane Road runs along what was the northern edge of

49. The former Plough at Crews Hill, now a private house. The picture cannot have been taken later than 1895, when Gripper's brewery (Tottenham) was taken over by Whitbread.

The Chase from **Cattlegate Road** to Cooper's Lane passing Hook Gate and Barvin Gate. The present name was in use by 1803.

Crews Hill

This is a small settlement on the extreme northern edge of Enfield close to the Hertfordshire border. The name derives from William Crew, one of the last keepers on Enfield Chase and later licensee of the Fallow Buck. Crews Hill Station was opened by the Great Northern Railway in 1910. After the First World War market gardening became profitable and resulted in a proliferation of glass-houses – there are still several large garden centres in the area. There has also been some limited housing development mainly in the angle between **Cattlegate Road** and Theobalds Park Road, but further expansion has so far been constrained by the Green Belt.

Cricket

By the early 19th century cricket was regularly played on Chase Green. Enfield Cricket Club was founded in 1856 and was widely supported by the local gentry. The first club captain was B.T. Bosanquet of **Clayesmore**, the father of **B J T Bosanquet** of Middlesex and England fame and inventor of the googly. Early years were marred by a rift within the club, a substantial body of members defecting to form the rival Enfield Amateur Cricket Club. (The two factions were later reunited.) Initially, the club used various grounds but settled at Lincoln Road in 1867, first as tenants, later acquiring the freehold.

There are several other long-established cricket clubs in Enfield. Cockfosters Cricket Club was founded in 1873 and enjoyed generous support from the **Bevan** family of Trent Park. The ground at Chalk Lane was leased from Cosmo Bevan, but in 1947 the freehold was acquired by Southgate Borough Council. North Enfield Cricket Club dates from 1886, and has played at Strayfield Road since 1954. Botany Bay Cricket Club was probably founded in 1900, but the earliest known score sheet dates from 1903.

Ernest Davies

Davies (1902-91) was Labour MP for Enfield (1945-50) and Enfield East (1950-59). A seasoned journalist and writer, he had had books published by the Left Book Club, and was widely regarded as an expert on the coal industry. He held a variety of junior ministerial posts under the Attlee government rising to Under Secretary of State at the Foreign Office (1950-51). During this time his counterpart in the House of Lords was Lord Henderson of Westgate (**William Henderson**) a former Labour MP for Enfield.

50. *J M Dent. Photo by Frederick Evans.*

In 1950, as a result of boundary changes, Davies moved to the new Enfield East constituency. Shortly before the 1959 General Election, with his wife seriously ill and not expected to live long, Davies decided to stand down and John Mackie was selected as Labour candidate in his place. Then Davies' wife made an unexpected recovery and he unsuccessfully sought another seat, being narrowly beaten for the Labour nomination at Barking by the notoriously libidinous Tom Driberg.

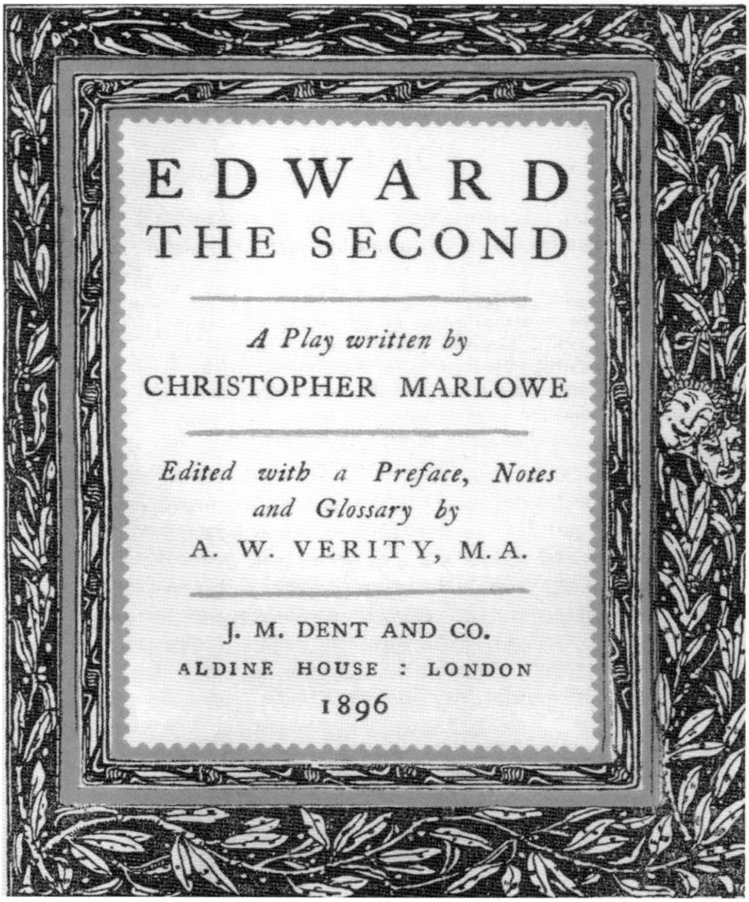

51. *Title page from J M Dent's Dramatists edition of Marlowe's* Edward II. *The book was bound by the author's great grandfather.*

Joseph Malaby Dent

One of the most innovative publishers of his generation, Dent (1849-1926) was the son of a Darlington house painter. After leaving school at thirteen, he was initially apprenticed to a printer but soon transferred his apprenticeship to a bookbinder. He came to London in 1867 and by 1872 had a bookbinding business in Hoxton, later moving to Great Eastern Street, Shoreditch. In 1888 he moved into publishing. He produced the 'Temple Classics', the 'Temple Dramatists', and the 'Temple Shakespeare', all well-produced pocket-sized volumes. From 1906 he published the influential 'Everyman's Library' series, well-printed editions of classic authors at affordable prices. In the first year of these Dent and his editor, Ernest Rhys, published a remarkable 153 titles. (The author's great grandfather, William Frederick Ford worked for J.M. Dent & Co as a foreman casemaker in the workshops at Great Eastern Street.) As the business grew, the office moved to Bedford Street, Covent Garden and the printing and bookbinding workshops to Letchworth.

Between 1910 and 1916 Dent lived at Hill Lodge, Clay Hill, Enfield. (The house was an early 19th century stuccoed building, standing immediately to the east of The Fallow Buck, which was demolished in 1965. In 1819 Hill Lodge had been the birthplace of the civil engineer, **Joseph Bazalgette**.)

52. isaac D'Israeli, who grew up at his father's home in Baker Street.

Isaac D'Israeli

Though famous in his lifetime, D'Israeli (1766-1848) has long been unjustly neglected and is now chiefly known as the father of Benjamin Disraeli. D'Israeli was born in the City of London into an affluent Sephardic Jewish family long connected with the Spanish and Portuguese Synagogue at Bevis Marks. His father owned a country house at Enfield and it was here that he spent much of his childhood. Ratebooks reveal that the house stood in Baker Street near the junction with Lancaster Road and was probably Carlton House, later a doctor's surgery, which lasted until demolition in 1965. According to Hodson and Ford's *History of Enfield* (1873), the D'Israeli family home was the house in Nag's Head Lane where John Clarke's School was later located. (This story must have emanated from Benjamin Disraeli, a notorious source of misinformation on his family history.) Isaac D'Israeli later quarrelled with the Bevis Marks Synagogue and had his children (including the future prime minister) baptised into the Church of England, a step that he was reluctant to take himself.

D'Israeli was an uncle of the distinguished architect, George Basevi, who designed the Fitzwilliam Museum at Cambridge and was later killed in a fall from the west tower of Ely Cathedral in 1847.

Duck Lees Lane

Called Duck Leys Lane in an auctioneer's catalogue of 1787, the name reflects the marshy nature of the ground and the close proximity of the River Lee. It originated as access to what

53. The gatehouse at Durants Arbour shortly before demolition in 1910.

was then marshland grazing. Since the closure of the railway level crossing access is now via Mollison Avenue rather than Scotland Green Road.

Durants Arbour

This was a large moated manor house of medieval origin formerly standing east of the Hertford Road slightly to the south of Durants Park and Enfield College. From the early 16th century through to 1671 it was the home of the influential **Wroth** family. It was later acquired by the Stringer family, one of whom, William Stringer, was married to a daughter of the notorious Judge Jeffreys. Much of the house was destroyed by fire in the late 18th century, but a substantial Tudor brick gatehouse *(ill. 53)* survived until demolished in 1910. The site has since been completely cleared and built over, but the filled-in moat has been the cause of many subsidence problems in the area.

East Enfield

East Enfield began as a series of small hamlets strung out along the Hertford Road. In 1572 Enfield Highway was known as Cocksmiths End. Close by, but still separate, was the small settlement of Green Street. To the north lay Enfield Wash, then known as Horsepoolstones, an early settlement which lay on the west side of the Hertford Road. On the east side ran the Turkey Brook, which followed the road as far south as Bell Lane. (The course was straightened in the early 19th century.) The small settlement at Turkey Street was already well established. The 1867 Ordnance Survey shows the area little changed, but by then thin ribbon development along the Hertford Road blurred the boundaries of the old settlements and there were buildings stretching from Green Street to the junction with Welches Lane (Ordnance Road).

In 1839 there were coaches twice daily from the White Lion, Old Road to London. These were supplemented by other coaches from as far away as Hertford and Cambridge which stopped on their way to London. In 1840 the first section of the railway from London to Cambridge was opened as far as Broxbourne. Initially there were no stations between Ponders End and Waltham Cross, but in 1855 Enfield Lock station (originally called Ordnance Factory) was opened. This was followed in 1884 by Brimsdown station. The Southbury Loop line (1891) gave the area another station, sited in Turkey Street. *(See separate entry for Railways)* This station lost its passenger service in 1909 as a result of tramway competition.

In the early 19th century an electric tramway was constructed along the Hertford Road. It reached the county boundary at Freezywater in 1907 and was completed to Waltham Cross in the following year, lasting until 1938 when it was converted to trolleybuses.

By 1831 the area had grown sufficiently to justify its own

54. An early 20th-century view of Hertford Road, Enfield Highway, showing St James's church and the police station.

55 Hertford Road, Enfield Wash, south of the Woolpack Bridge, c.1905.

parish church (St James). Much of the early housing development was linked with the employees of the Royal Small Arms Factory. In the angle between Ordnance Road and Hertford Road, Grove Road and Alma Road (both now demolished) were developed from the mid 1850s, and Medcalf Road and Warwick Road were built in the early 1860s. The Putney Lodge Estate (Mandeville Road, Totteridge Road etc.) was built from 1867. By 1914 the Ordnance Road area was developed as was the Hertford Road from St James church to just south of Bullsmoor Lane.

The best grazing land in Enfield was on the Lee Marshes. Many of the former access roads to the marshes survive today: Bell Lane, Pigots Lane (Carterhatch Road), Millmarsh Lane and Stockingswater Lane. The area later became a centre of market gardening. Even as late as the mid 1930s there were glasshouses in large numbers.

Brickmaking was once a major industry in the area. The last brickworks (in Hoe Lane) closed as late as the 1970s. The Royal Small Arms Factory was built at Enfield Lock from 1814, coming into production in 1816. The factory was originally powered by waterwheels driven by the River Lee and raw materials and finished weapons were transported by barge. The workers there formed something of a working class elite in East Enfield: the factory had a trade union branch as early as 1855 and the workers were responsible for setting up the Enfield Highway Co-operative Society in 1872.

Housing development resumed after the First World War, but there was still open land in the Hoe Lane and Turkey Street areas.

Two large council estates were developed: the Albany Estate (from 1926) and the Suffolks Estate (from 1930), and more were built after the war, in particular, the Elsinge Estate on market-garden land between Turkey Street and Bullsmoor Lane.

East Enfield today presents an uneven picture. In Hertford Road, Turkey Street and Green Street a few buildings survive from the 18th century and earlier, but the dominant impression is of an uneasy mixture of styles from mid-Victorian through to the 1970s. The recent closure of the Royal Small Arms Factory enabled much development on the site: the so-called Enfield Island Village, with a few remnants of the factory incorporated to pacify the conservationists.

East Lodge

An early Victorian house on the site of one of the old lodges of Enfield Chase, it stands on the south side of East Lodge Lane close to the junction with The Ridgeway. For many years the home of the Cranfield family, it has had a chequered history in more recent years and was for a time occupied by squatters.

East Lodge Lane

This was once a trackway across The Chase linking **The Ridgeway** with Cattlegate Road. The name derives from East Lodge, a former lodge on The Chase. Before the enclosure of The Chase in 1777, the road continued west of The Ridgeway to link up with Wagon Road.

Edmonton Hundred Historical Society

Enfield's principal local history society was founded in 1936 to promote the study of local history in the former Edmonton Hundred of Middlesex (i.e. Tottenham, Wood Green, Edmonton, Southgate, Enfield, Monken Hadley, Potters Bar and South Mimms). It was disbanded during the last war but revived in 1949. In its early days the Society also carried out archaeological investigations, including an excavation of a Roman site at Churchfields, Edmonton, but the archaeological wing subsequently broke away to form the core of **Enfield Archaeological Society**.

The Society expanded greatly after 1958, when David Pam became secretary. Its main achievement has been in publications, producing a series of high quality occasional papers of which no less than sixty-four have been published over the last forty years.

The Society's membership was originally mainly from Tottenham and Edmonton. However the reduction of the white middle class in these two areas has seen the Society's membership and activities shift towards Enfield and Southgate. Since 1978 the Society has had a Jewish Research Group with its own meetings and publications programme.

Enfield Archaeological Society

Founded in 1955 by Geoffrey Gillam, who was to serve for many years as chairman and who had previously carried out archaeological investigations under the auspices of the **Edmonton Hundred Historical Society.** The Society has carried out excavations on a prehistoric earthwork on Bush Hill, the site of Elsing in the grounds of Forty Hall and a Roman site in Bush Hill Park. In addition it has performed rescue work and many keyhole excavations in Enfield gardens. Its publications include *Prehistoric and Roman Enfield* (1973), *Enfield at War 1914-1918*, *Enfield at War 1939-1945*, *Theatres, Music Halls and Cinemas in the London Borough of Enfield* (1986), *Forty Hall* (1997) – all written by Geoffrey Gillam – and *Royal Palaces of Enfield* (1984) by Ian Jones and Ivy Drayton.

Enfield Chase

The Chase was formerly a large tract of woodland in the north-west corner of Enfield. The Domesday Survey of 1086 records that in Enfield there was woodland sufficient to sustain 2000 pigs and a similar amount of woodland in Edmonton, suggesting that the area may have been managed in common by the two parishes. By 1136 the de Mandeville fam-

56. The Enfield Chase enclosure map of 1777.

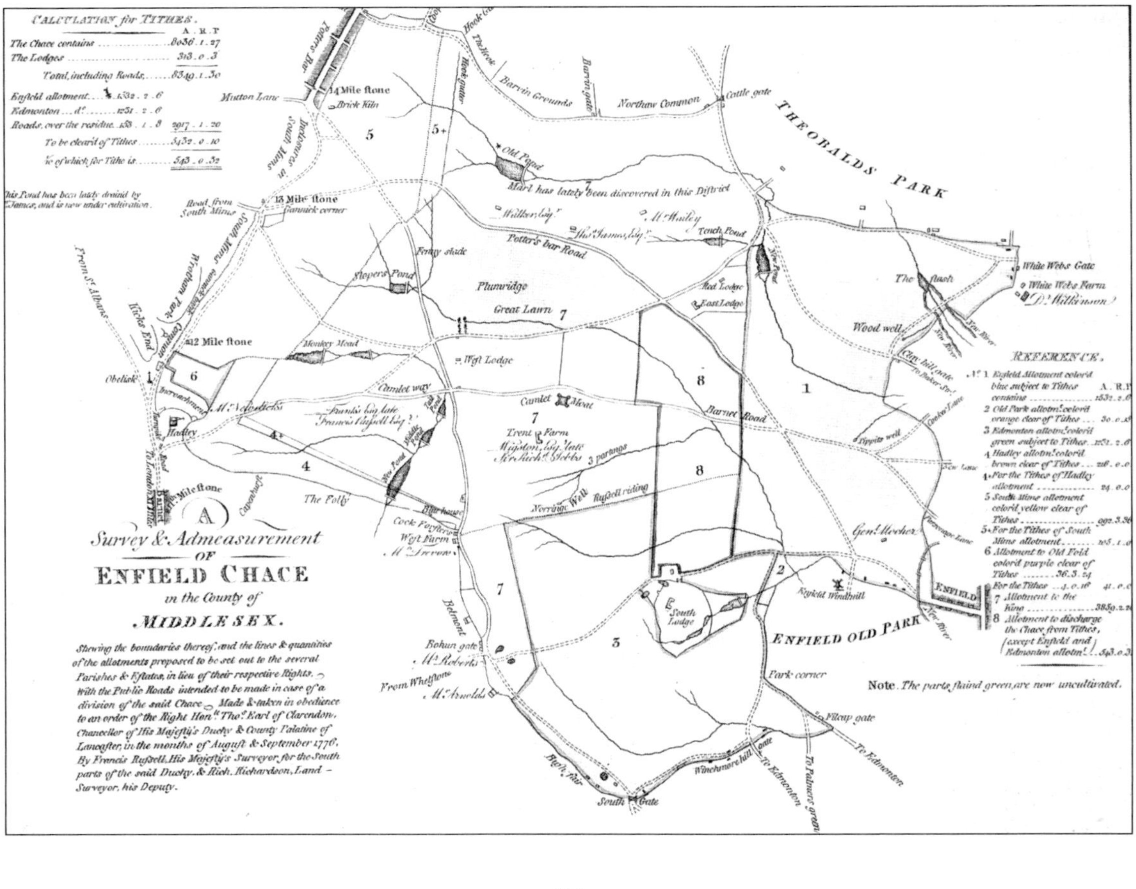

ANNO DECIMO SEPTIMO

Georgii III. Regis.

C A P. XVII.

An Act for dividing the Chase of *Enfield*, in the County of *Middlesex*; and for other Purposes therein mentioned.

HEREAS the King's most Excellent Majesty is seised to himself, his Heirs and Successors, in Fee-simple, of the Chase of Enfield, lying within the Parish of Enfield, in the County of Middlesex, being Parcel of the Estates and Possessions of the Duchy of Lancaster, subject nevertheless to such Right of Common, and other Rights, as the Freeholders and Copyholders of Messuages, Lands, and Tenements, situate and being within the several Parishes of Enfield, Edmonton, South Mimms, and Monken Hadley, in the said County of Middlesex, or the Tenants and Occupiers thereof for the Time being, are intitled unto, within and upon the said Chase: And whereas the Master, Fellows, and Scholars of Trinity College in the University of Cambridge are Patrons of the Vicarage of Enfield aforesaid, and also Owners of

57. Title page of the Enfield Chase enclosure Act of 1777.

ily had transformed the area into a semi-private hunting ground. Control passed from them to the de Bohuns and, on the extinction of this family's male line, to the Duchy of Lancaster - Henry Bolingbroke, Duke of Lancaster (later King Henry IV) had married Mary de Bohun. Enfield Chase thus became a royal hunting ground.

In 1656, during the Commonwealth period, Enfield Chase was enclosed and parts sold to former officers in the Parliamentary army. This resulted in tension between the new landowners and local people who had exercised grazing rights on the Chase, spilling over into violence in 1659 when the commoners deliberately broke down hedges and fences and drove cattle into fields of growing crops. In 1660, with the restoration of the monarchy, Enfield Chase reverted to the Duchy of Lancaster. The final years of Enfield Chase were marred by massive theft of timber, poaching of the king's deer, and corrupt officialdom. In 1777 the Chase was enclosed by Act of Parliament and parts of it were allocated to the parishes of Edmonton, South Mimms and Monken Hadley in lieu of lost grazing rights. The land was mostly cleared for agriculture - remnants of the original vegetation can be seen on Hadley Common and the Trent Park Estate. Much of Cockfosters, Hadley Wood and the northern part of Southgate have been built on former Chase land.

Enfield Court

This was a substantial property on the west side of Baker Street: it has a 17th-century core with many later additions. From 1852 until his death in 1915 it was the home of **Col. Sir Alfred Somerset**. His executors sold the house to become the Lower School of Enfield Grammar School. A circular riding house in the grounds, built by Somerset and once a favourite venue for band concerts and other social events, was demolished after bomb damage during the last war.

Enfield Grammar School

Enfield's Grammar School originated in a pre-Reformation chantry foundation at St Andrew's church. Some sort of school was in being by 1507, and it managed to survive the dissolution of chantries in 1547. The earliest part of the present buildings dates from the 1590s; these were extended in 1883 and later.

In 1894 the school received its first grant from Middlesex County Council. In 1924 the house called **Enfield Court** was acquired for use as a lower school.

There was conflict between headmasters and the Vestry during the 19th century. The Rev. John Milne, appointed in 1791, was accused in 1818 of wholesale beatings of the boys and the Vestry voted to dismiss

58. Enfield Court, then the home of Sir Alfred Somerset, now the lower school of Enfield Grammar School.

59. An Enfield Grammar School prize giving shortly after the First World War. The then headmaster, Edwin Mortimer Eagles (right), according to a former pupil, Hugh Jenkins, kept a formidable collection of canes in his study.

60. The original building of Enfield Grammar School (still in use) dating from c.1590.

him. He retaliated by bringing a court action against the Vestry, and won. Milne remained headmaster until 1830, when he resigned amid accusations of irregularities in the registers.

His successor, James Emery, was accused of neglecting his duties and in 1846 he was dismissed. However, he refused to leave his living accommodation until bribed. His successor, Charles Chambers, though beginning well, fell out of favour by becoming Vicar's warden to the **Rev. John Moore Heath** who had infuriated the parish with his secretive dismantling of the ancient church pews. The school's fortunes revived under William Ridewood, headmaster for over thirty years, retiring in 1908. It was gradually brought into the state system, accepting its first grant in 1893.

The school became a comprehensive in 1967, despite a stubborn rearguard action fought in the courts by a group of parents, and was amalgamated with the former Chase Boys School. The two schools separated in 1970 and Enfield Grammar reverted to its original name, though remaining a comprehensive.

Enfield Manor House

Often called Enfield Palace, the Manor House stood in Church Street directly opposite St Andrew's Church. Originally owned by the de Mandeville and de Bohun families, its ownership passed in 1419 to the Duchy of Lancaster. Prints from the 18th century show a substantial E-plan house almost certainly of 16th-century date, much of it of timber-framed construction. In the late 17th century the building was let to Dr Robert Uvedale, who ran a boys' boarding school and was also responsible for planting a cedar of Lebanon (then very uncommon in England) in the grounds. By the late 18th century the building was in a dilapidated state and all but one wing was demolished. The surviving remnant was used at different times as a boys' boarding school, a Post Office and the first home of the Enfield Town Constitutional Club (now in Old Park Avenue). In 1928 the building suffered the ultimate indignity of being demolished to make way

61. Enfield Manor House (or Palace) showing the building complete.

62. The surviving wing of the Manor House prior to demolition in 1928.

for Pearson's department store. Dr Uvedale's cedar, by then a substantial and impressive tree, was felled.

Enfield Preservation Society

Enfield's leading conservation and amenity society grew out of the vociferous protests generated in 1935 when Enfield Urban District Council proposed to build a town hall on Chase Green. The Society was formed early in 1936 with Geoffrey Daisley, the then vicar of St Andrew's Church, as chairman. Early in 1937 the Council abandoned plans to build on Chase Green only to propose an equally unpopular scheme, namely to sell off the Library Green to build shops. Pressure from the Society forced a public enquiry, which the Council lost.

During the last war the Society went into abeyance and was not revived until 1959. Its profile rose as it fought a long and hard battle against the Council's plans for pedestrianisation of Enfield Town. This plan first surfaced in 1961 as a solution to car parking and traffic congestion and would have involved an inner ring road cutting through St Andrew's churchyard and Holly Walk and subjecting Enfield Grammar School and Enfield County School to noise and pollution. The battle continued until 1967, when the then Minister of Housing and Local Government, Anthony Greenwood, acting on the advice of a junior minister, Lord Kennett, rejected the scheme.

The Society has had an active publications programme responsible for (among other things) David Pam's authoritative 3-volume *History of Enfield* (1990-94), the same author's *Story of Enfield Chase* (1984) and Valerie Carter's *Treasures of Enfield* (2000).

Since 1988 the Society has had its headquarters at Jubilee Hall, Parsonage Lane. This is essentially a First World War army hut, latterly used for warehousing, but it has been refurbished to a high standard.

The leading personalities in the Society have included Valerie Carter (chairman and then president and the driving force behind the publications programme), Carinthia Arbuthnot Lane (secretary

1959-67 and president 1988-94, largely responsible for the Society's post-war revival) and Irene Smith (secretary 1969-96, a strong personality with formidable organisational skills).

Enfield Road

A former trackway across The Chase linking Windmill Hill to Cockfosters, it was known as East Barnet Road in 1803. The middle section was re-named Enfield Road in 1932. The eastern end was known as Slades Hill by 1874, named after the Slade family, licensees of the Jolly Farmers for many years. The western end, where it runs through Southgate, was renamed Bramley Road in 1934, after the Bramley family of West Pole Farm.

Enfield Town

Enfield Town was the largest settlement in the parish and was also the administrative and religious centre. At the time of the Domesday Survey (1086) Enfield had a priest, implying that there must have been a church, almost certainly on the site of St Andrew's Church. (The oldest part of the present building dates back to the 13th century.) Much of the basic street layout was established by 1572, with a village green in the centre – this was progressively encroached upon, ultimately leaving only a small paved area where the fountain now stands.

Enfield Town was an important trading centre from an early date. The first market charter was granted in 1303, but it is not clear how effective this was. In the late 16th century a Sunday meat market was held, resulting in conflict with the Church authorities. The present market traces its origins to a charter granted in 1618. In 1632 the parish purchased a house called The Vine, demolished it and created the Market Place on the site. The market was initially very successful, but began to decline in the late 18th century, and closed soon after 1798. There was an unsuccessful attempt to revive it in the mid 1820s, but it was resurrected in the late 19th century and continues to this day.

Enfield's first railway, the Lea Valley Line (1840), gave Enfield Town a wide berth, the nearest station being at Ponders End, but in 1849 a single track branch line was built from Water Lane (Angel Road) to a terminus in Nag's Head Lane (Southbury Road) on the site of the present Enfield Town Station. In 1872 the route to London was considerably shortened by means of a new line via Bethnal Green and Hackney Downs to Lower Edmonton. In 1871 the Great Northern Railway opened its station on Windmill Hill, the terminus of a branch line from Wood Green. This was replaced in 1910 by the present Enfield Chase Station when the line was extended to Cuffley.

Enfield Town was also the

63. Enfield Town in the late 19th century. The Greyhound Inn (centre) was demolished in 1897 to make way for the London & Provincial Bank (now Barclay's).

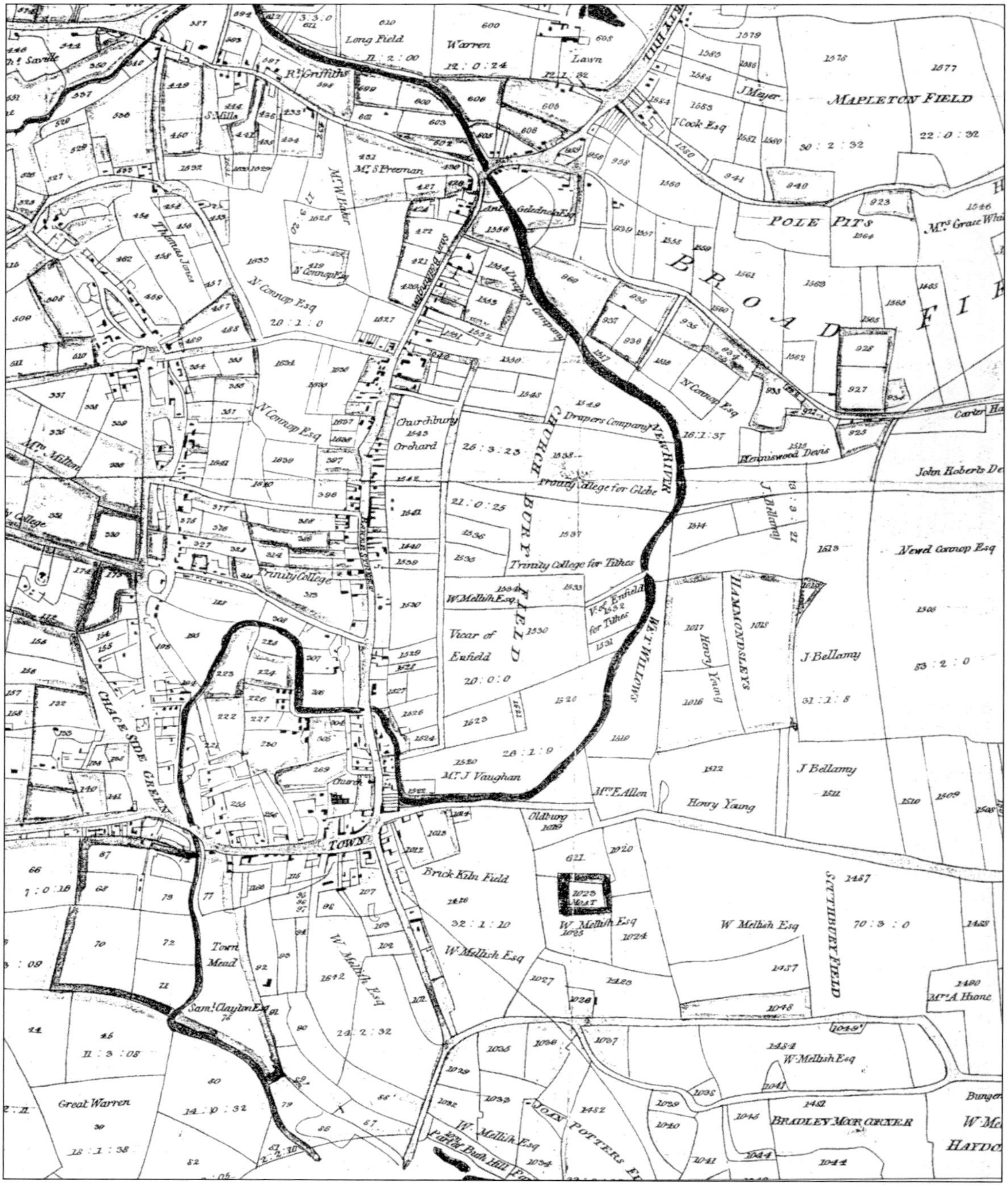

64. The Enfield Town area on the enclosure map of 1803.

65. An early 20th-century view of the Market Place. The picture was taken between the rebuilding of the King's Head (1899) and the removal of the Market Cross (1904).

terminus of two electric tramways. The line from Palmers Green and Winchmore Hill (via Village Road and Park Avenue) opened in 1909. This was followed in 1911 by a line from Ponders End (via Southbury Road). In 1938 the route to Palmers Green and Winchmore Hill was converted to trolleybuses, while the Southbury Road route was completely abandoned. The trolleybuses were phased out in 1961.

Suburban development began shortly after the opening of the first railway station in 1849. The first major development was Enfield New Town (Raleigh Road, Essex Road, Sydney Road and Cecil Road), built up from 1852. This was a mixed development with large houses in London Road and Essex Road and small workmen's cottages in Sydney Road and Raleigh Road. To the east of Chase Side the Gordon House Estate was developed slowly from 1858. In the Lancaster Road area the Woodlands Estate, the Cedars Estate and the Birkbeck Estate were all constructed from the late 1870s.

The Great Northern Railway tended to attract a much better class of commuter than its rival, the Great Eastern Railway, and the Windmill Hill area saw some up-market housing developments. The Bycullah Estate (1879), the Old Park Estate (1880) and the Glebe Estate (1880) consisted mainly of large detached houses.

After the First World War housing development resumed, covering much former orchard and market garden land. This included the huge Willow Estate, stretching from Southbury Road to Carterhatch Lane, developed from the mid 1930s. The Cockfosters extension of the Piccadilly Line resulted in more building to the west of Enfield Town in the Slades Hill/Enfield Road area. By 1939 the district was virtually fully developed with the gap between Enfield Town and the rest of the London conurbation closed and the built-up area extending as far north as Forty Hill.

In the post-war period Green Belt restrictions have so far prevented major expansion, although there have been numerous small infills and many large houses in the Ridgeway/ Windmill Hill area have been demolished to make way for blocks of flats.

For many years after the last war Enfield Town's shopping centre was in obvious decline and plans for an inner ring-road (now abandoned) did little to encourage investment. Things changed dramatically in 1982 with the opening of the Palace Gardens Shopping Precinct, as a result of which the fortunes of Enfield Town were revived. Whether the second phase of the Palace Gardens Precinct (Palace Exchange – opened late in 2006) will have a similar effect remains to be seen.

Enfield Town is now a place of great contrasts. St Andrew's Church, Gentleman's Row and the Grammar School rub shoulders slightly uneasily with the Palace Gardens Precinct and the Civic Centre.

Ermine Street

Ermine Street was the Roman road from London to York. Its line can be followed from Bishopsgate to the Tottenham/ Edmonton boundary along Kingsland Road, Stoke Newington High Street, Stamford Hill and Tottenham High Road. North of this point the alignment has been largely lost until it re-appears at Bulls Cross, from where it can be followed across the Hertfordshire boundary into the Theobalds Estate. In Edmonton, Victoria Road (Hyde Lane) follows the suspected alignment. North of Lincoln Road the road can be traced on old field boundaries on the Breton Estate Map (1785) leading in a north-westerly direction towards Bulls Cross. The otherwise inexplicable kink in Lincoln Road immediately west of the A10 is clearly the point where Ermine Street once crossed.

Thomas Fermor-Hesketh

Fermor-Hesketh (1881-1944) was briefly Conservative MP for Enfield from 1922 to 1923. He was a successful Lancashire businessman, who had been educated at Eton and Sandhurst and had served in the Horse Guards. He lost his seat in 1924 to **William Henderson** of the Labour Party and never stood again for Enfield, but he eventually returned to Parliament as Lord Hesketh.

Sir Ambrose Fleming

Fleming (1849-1945) was an eminent electrical engineer. Acting as a consultant for Ediswan, he carried out research into carbon filament light bulbs which led almost accidentally to the invention of thermionic valves – the patent was filed in 1904. (Much of the research work was carried out at the Ediswan factory at Ponders End.) Thermionic valves were a vital component in radio, television, radar and computers – the whole of modern electronics was initially dependent on this invention. In his later years Fleming assisted John Logie Baird in the development of television. In 1962 an Enfield boys' technical grammar school was named after him, but this has since been closed so that its buildings could be appropriated by Enfield College. There is now nothing to commemorate Fleming in Enfield.

Viscount Folkestone, William Pleydell-Bouverie

Folkestone (1841-1900) was Conservative MP for Enfield (1885-89) – he was the first MP to represent the new Enfield Parliamentary Division when it was created. He had previously been MP for South Wiltshire (1874-85). His tenure of the Enfield seat was brief, cut short in 1889 by his elevation to the House of Lords as the 5th Earl of Radnor on the death of his father.

Football

Enfield Football Club was founded by John Bruce Skinner in 1893 as the Enfield Spartans. (An earlier Enfield Football Club had fallen by the wayside.) The club's first pitch was on Bailey's Field – off Baker Street, close to the Jolly Butchers. They then moved to a field at the northern end of the Churchbury Lane rented from Mr Tucker, a local dairyman, and then on to a field on the east side of Churchbury Lane now covered by Orchard Way. When the club was revived after the First World War it was found that the ground had been ploughed up and the cost of restoring it would have been prohibitive. The club came close to extinction at this point, but re-established itself on a field at the northern end of Churchbury Lane close to the second ground it had occupied. In 1936 it moved to a purpose-built stadium in Southbury Road leased from Enfield Council, where it was to remain until 1997 when the site was controversially sold for housing development.

The recent history of Enfield

66. *Enfield Football Club's stadium in Southbury Road, newly-built in 1936. The ground was sold for building in 1997.*

FC has been a troubled one with the loss of its ground (effectively rendering the team homeless), so much so that rebellious supporters have formed a rival team, Enfield Town FC.

For about 50 years in the last century Enfield Football Club were in the Athenian League and in 1962 won its first league title. A second title in 1963 brought them promotion to the Isthmian League and here they won seven more league titles. They were one of the first two Isthmian teams to join what is now the Conference League. They were relegated to the Isthmian again in 1990 but despite success there over a number of years were not permitted promotion to the Conference due to doubts over the club's financial standing.

The club won the FA Amateur Cup in 1966-7 and 1969-70.

Edward Ford

Ford (1814-1893) was the author with **George Hodson** of *A History of Enfield* (1873). He was born at Lancaster and settled in Enfield after marrying Elizabeth Lewis, the daughter and heiress of T. Winchester Lewis of Old Park, Bush Hill (now the Bush Hill Park Golf Club). Ford was a man of refined and scholarly tastes and was assisted in his research work by his son, John Walker Ford. His work is still useful today provided that readers make due allowances for the biases and prejudices of the era in which it was written. John Walker Ford wrote *A Sketch towards a History of the neighbourhood: being some particulars of Bush Hill Park*. This fascinating compilation, now very rare, was printed in a small edition in 1904 for sale at a fund raising event for St Stephen's church, Bush Hill Park.

Forty Hall

This is a substantial Jacobean mansion built 1629-32 for **Sir Nicholas Rainton** and although much altered, still retains original plasterwork and woodwork. After Rainton's death it passed to a nephew, also called Nicholas Rainton, and then to the Wolstenholme and Breton families. The house was purchased 1787 by Edmund Armstrong, whose heirs, pressed by creditors, sold up in 1799. The new owner was James Meyer a wealthy merchant of Dutch extraction, whose family remained at Forty Hall until 1895. The house was then purchased by H.C.B. Bowles of Myddelton House for his son **Henry Bowles**. On his death in 1943 the property passed to a grandson, Derek Parker Bowles, who sold it in 1951 to Enfield Council. *His* son, Andrew Parker Bowles, was married to Camilla, now the Duchess of Cornwall and the wife of the Prince of Wales.

The house is now a museum and the grounds a public park.

67. *Forty Hall in 1894 shortly before the death of James Meyer. The two young girls in the boat are Meyer's daughters.*

68. *The entrance to the stable yard at Forty Hall. The figures on the left are James Meyer and his wife.*

Forty Hill

By 1572 there were several settlements established in this part of Enfield. Forty Hill was then known as Forty Green. There were cottages in Bulls Cross Lane (now Bulls Cross) and there were two small settlements in Whitewebbs Lane – Romey Street (at the Bulls Cross end) and Whitewebbs proper (near the King and Tinker). In Clay Hill lay the settlement of Bridge Street (near where the Rose and Crown now stands).

The focal point of Forty Hill in the 16th century was the great house of Elsing which lay between the site of Forty Hall and the Turkey Brook. This belonged to Sir Thomas Lovell, Chancellor of the Exchequer to Henry VII, and it became a royal palace in 1539. It was here in 1547 that Edward VI was told of the death of his father (Henry VIII) and of his own accession to the throne. Although Queen Elizabeth stayed at Elsing on several occasions, the property was not particularly well maintained and by the early 17th century was in a parlous state. It was still standing in 1656, but appears to have been demolished shortly after this date. The remains were partially excavated in the 1960s by the **Enfield Archaeological Society**.

The course of the **New River** through the Forty Hill area was drastically altered in 1859 with the abandonment of a huge Loop through the Whitewebbs Estate and its replacement by a new section running from Turkey Street to Tenniswood Road. Substantial remains of the old

69. *A late 19th-century view of Forty Hill showing Worcester Lodge and the Goat. The licence was transferred to a new building at Forty Hill Green.*

70. Forty Hill Green c.1960 showing The Goat, built in 1928 to replace the original pub in Forty Hill. (This is currently being converted into flats.) The buses were diverted to Carterhatch Lane in 1971.

loop can be seen in the Whitewebbs and Gough Park Estates including an early 19th century cast iron aqueduct in Flash Lane.

Forty Hall was built from 1629. Other great houses in the area included **Whitewebbs** (1791, for Dr Abraham Wilkinson), **Capel House** (1793) and **Myddelton House** (1818).

By the mid-19th century the basic layout and disposition of the settlements was not much changed since 1572. Remote from public transport, the area was unattractive to commuters and grew little during the 19th century. Jesus Church was built in 1835, paid for by the Meyer family of Forty Hall, and a National School was erected in 1851 close to Maidens Bridge.

Communications in the Forty Hill area have never been particularly good. The nearest railway stations are at Turkey Street (opened 1891, closed 1909, re-opened 1960) and at Gordon Hill and Crews Hill (both opened 1910). Road access was considerably improved after 1924 with the opening of the **Great Cambridge Road** (A10). This has become even more important in recent years with the creation of the M25: the two roads intersect at a junction to the north of Bullsmoor Lane.

In 1868 the Bridgen Hall Estate, a large tract of land between Carterhatch Lane and Goat Lane, was sold for building. The streets laid out were St George's Road, Garnault Road, Russell Road, Layard Road and Bridgenhall Road, but development, mainly in the form of workmen's cottages, was slow – there were vacant plots on this estate well into the 1930s. In addition, gravel digging took place on parts of the estate resulting in later subsidence problems.

By 1914 the Forty Hill/Bulls Cross area was still predominantly rural and, apart from some rather slow progress on the Bridgen Hall Estate, was still largely undeveloped. There was still open country separating Forty Hill from Enfield Town.

The local authority, showing remarkable foresight, acquired land for use as public open space. The North Enfield Recreation Ground (Tucker's Fields) was purchased in 1907, followed by Hilly Fields in 1911. This policy was continued after the First World War, notably in 1931 with the purchase of the Whitewebbs Estate from Sir Duncan Orr-Lewis.

By 1939 the Forty Hill area was solidly linked to the rest of the London conurbation. North of Forty Hill, however, it remained essentially rural and the Green Belt policy has so far restricted any further major developments in this area.

After the last war two large council estates were built: to the north of Hoe Lane and between Turkey Street and Bullsmoor Lane. These were accompanied by the erection of two new primary schools Worcesters (1954) and Capel Manor (1958). More public open space was secured when the local authority purchased the Forty Hall Estate in 1951. In 1971 the construction of a short section of road, linking Myddelton Avenue to Baker Street, enabled most through traffic to be diverted away from Forty Hill and Maidens Bridge.

Today the Forty Hill and Bulls Cross area is in a curious half and half state. To the south it is firmly locked on to London. To the north, the intrusion of such urban oriented facilities as sports grounds, riding schools and garden centres, bears witness to a process of creeping urbanisation.

Sir John French

French (1852-1925) was Commander of the British Expeditionary Force in France from 1914. Criticised for bad judgment and indecisiveness, he was replaced by Sir Douglas Haig late in 1915. For some years prior to the war, he lived at The Manor House (now demolished), which stood at the junction of Whitewebbs Lane and Bulls Cross, and which he rented from the Theobalds Estate. His son, Gerald French, writing in 1930, implied that this was a family home, but Richard Holmes in *The Little Field Marshal* (1981) suggests more convincingly, that as Sir John's marriage was by this time in decline, his appearances at Enfield were mainly at weekends and that he spent more time at his West End flat, which suited his lifestyle rather better. His sons were actively involved in the Enfield Cricket Club.

Gentleman's Row

This distinguished row originated as a path along the eastern boundary of The Chase; the name reflects the continued affluence of the neighbourhood. Despite their Georgian façades, several of the houses have substantial remains of 16th-century timber framing within. The road was sometimes known as Archway Road and Archway Place from the former Archway Tavern, now Archway House. The Row contains some of the finest houses in Enfield and can be compared favourably with Chiswick Mall, Strand on the Green and Harrow on the Hill.

Goat Lane

This road is named from a pub which stood on the corner with Forty Hill. (There was also a Goat Lane in Ponders End, similarly named after a pub, which now forms part of Queensway.)

Goldsdown Road

This is a former access road to some grazing land on the marshes; it was known as Lower Water Lane in 1775 and Water Lane in 1803. (Angel Road, Edmonton, in a similarly low-lying area, was once called Water Lane.) The present name, adopted in1903, is derived from an old field to the north of Green Street.

71. Archway House, Gentleman's Row. The view is now impeded by cars parked on what was once the front garden.

72. *Gentleman's Row, Enfield's finest street. Many of the houses have timber framing concealed behind Georgian brickwork.*

73. *A late 19th-century view of Goat Lane.*

Gordon Road

This was originally a cul-de-sac off Baker Street called either Fighting Cocks Lane (from a former pub) or Gordon Lane (from Gordon House). After the demolition of Gordon House, the road was extended to Chase Side and renamed Gordon Road.

Grange Park

This residential district straddles the former Southgate/Enfield border and is built on land once part of the Old Park Estate. Between 1907 and 1914 development took place in Grange Drive (Green Dragon Lane), Old Park Ridings, The Chine and The Grangeway. The builder was Richard Metherell, originally from North Devon, who had previously worked in the Muswell Hill area. The houses are large and well-designed and the layout spacious. The population was and has remained overwhelmingly middle class. Grange Park Station (1910) remained the area's only link with the outside world until 1972, when the W9 bus was introduced.

Great Cambridge Road (A10)

This road originated in plans drawn up in 1912 for a network of arterial roads in and around London. The first part ran from Tottenham to Wormley with the intention of by-passing the already congested Hertford Road. Construction began at the Tottenham end soon after the end of the First World War and by 1924 had reached Carterhatch Lane. It was built with a single carriageway, but the planners had the prescience to leave room for a second in case it should be needed. Work on a second carriageway was halted by the outbreak of war, by which time work had been completed from Tottenham as far as the Cambridge Roundabout. Dualling the road through Enfield was

74. *A newly-built section of the Great Cambridge Road, probably near Church Street, Edmonton.*

75. The Great Cambridge Road under construction c.1922.

completed in 1965. By-passes for Hoddesdon and Ware were built in the 1970s, but plans for a southern extension from Tottenham to Newington Green were abandoned.

Green Dragon Lane

The road's name derives from the Green Dragon, which stood at the junction of Green Lanes and Green Dragon Lane – the pub later moved to its present site on the corner of Green Lanes and Vicars Moor Lane. At different times the Lane was known variously as Filcaps Lane (Filcaps Farm stood nearby), Chase Lane, Old Park Lane and Dog Kennel Lane.

Sir Nigel Gresley

Gresley (1876-1941) was an eminent railway engineer. He trained at the Crewe Works of the London & North Western Railway, before moving to the Horwich Works of the Lancashire & Yorkshire Railway as a pupil of Sir John Aspinall. He later moved to the Doncaster Works of the Great Northern Railway, being appointed as the company's Locomotive Engineer in 1911. On the formation of the London & North Eastern Railway in 1923 Gresley was appointed as Chief Mechanical Engineer to the new company, a post which he held until his death. The high point of his career came in 1938, when one of his locomotives (*Mallard* of the A4 class) achieved a world speed record for steam traction of 126 mph, which remains unbeaten to this day.

In 1923, when his office was transferred from Doncaster to King's Cross, he moved to Camlet House, Hadley Wood, where he remained until his wife died in 1929. He was a founder member of the Hadley Wood Golf Club and rose to be club captain. A fellow club member, the interior designer, Sir Charles Allom, was employed by Gresley as a consultant in the design of new restaurant cars for the LNER.

Radclyffe Hall

Margeurite Radclyffe Hall (1880-1943) was a lesbian who made no secret of her sexuality, living openly with her partner, Lady Una Troubridge. For two years between January 1919 and 1921 the couple lived at Chipchase, a large house in Camlet Way, Hadley Wood. (Among their neighbours was Bramwell Booth, General of the Salvation Army, who lived nearby in Lancaster Avenue. Whether they ever met and

76. Sir Nigel Gresley's finest product, Mallard *of the A4 class, which in 1938 achieved a world speed record (for a steam locomotive) of 126 mph.*

77. Radclyffe Hall in 1928.

whether they had anything significant to say to each other is unfortunately unrecorded.) Her best known work, now appearing rather dated, was *The Well of Loneliness* (1928) published in a limited edition by Jonathan Cape. Its account of a lesbian relationship did not become famous until the evangelical editor of the *Sunday Express* declared that "I would rather give a healthy boy or a healthy girl a phial of prussic acid than this novel." He called on the Home Secretary to ban the book, which a compliant William Joynson-Hicks did. However, Cape had had the foresight to send moulds of the type to Paris where it was reprinted in a new edition. When the matter came to court, the book was banned.

The Well was republished in 1949 without legal opposition, and has remained in print since. Indeed, in 1974 it was read as the BBC Radio Four's *Book at Bedtime.*

Thomas Hardy

The connection of Thomas Hardy (1840-1928) with Enfield came through his second wife, Florence Emily Dugdale (1879-1937), an Enfield schoolmistress and the daughter of a long-serving headmaster of St Andrew's School. She was born in Sydney Road, the family later moving to a house at River Front off Southbury Road. Florence nourished literary ambitions and managed to produce some children's books and short stories of questionable quality. Her most substantial offering was *Tim's Sister*, a children's book, heavily moralistic and mawkish in tone and not much to modern taste. It is clear that she met Hardy well before the death of Hardy's first wife, Emma, a fact that he subsequently went to great lengths to conceal. However, soon after the death of Emma late in 1912, Florence moved into Max Gate, Hardy's home near Dorchester, and the couple were married on 10th February 1914 at St Andrew's Church, Enfield Town. A report of the wedding in the *Enfield Gazette*, described Hardy as the 'world's greatest living novelist', a compliment but something of an overstatement since Henry James, Joseph Conrad and Marcel Proust were all still alive at the time.

Soon after Hardy's death in 1928 there was published a two-volume biography apparently written by Florence. However, although the manuscript was typed by Florence, it has now been established that it was almost entirely written by Hardy himself prior to his death. All that Florence contributed was a final chapter and the deletion of all favourable references to Hardy's first wife, Emma. Despite being nearly forty years younger than Hardy, Florence outlived him by only nine years, dying at the age of fifty-eight.

78. John Moore Heath, vicar of Enfield 1844-70.

John Moore Heath

Heath (1808-82) was a contentious vicar of St Andrew's Church, Enfield from 1844 to 1870. He was born in Holborn, the son of a barrister, and was educated at Westminster School and Trinity College, Cambridge. He would have liked to have followed his father into the legal profession, but this was precluded by deafness and he opted instead for the Church, being ordained deacon in 1836 and priest in 1838. While at Cambridge he had been influenced by the High Church movement, a seed that was to bear some very bitter fruit.

Heath was appointed to Enfield in 1844, soon after the death of the previous incumbent, Daniel Cresswell. The early part of his incumbency was apparently peaceful, but beneath the surface tensions were mounting. In 1853 Heath had plans prepared for a complete re-pewing of the church, which involved the removal of the old box pews. Fearing opposition in the parish, Heath did not consult the Vestry, did not apply to the Bishop for a faculty, and raised the funds

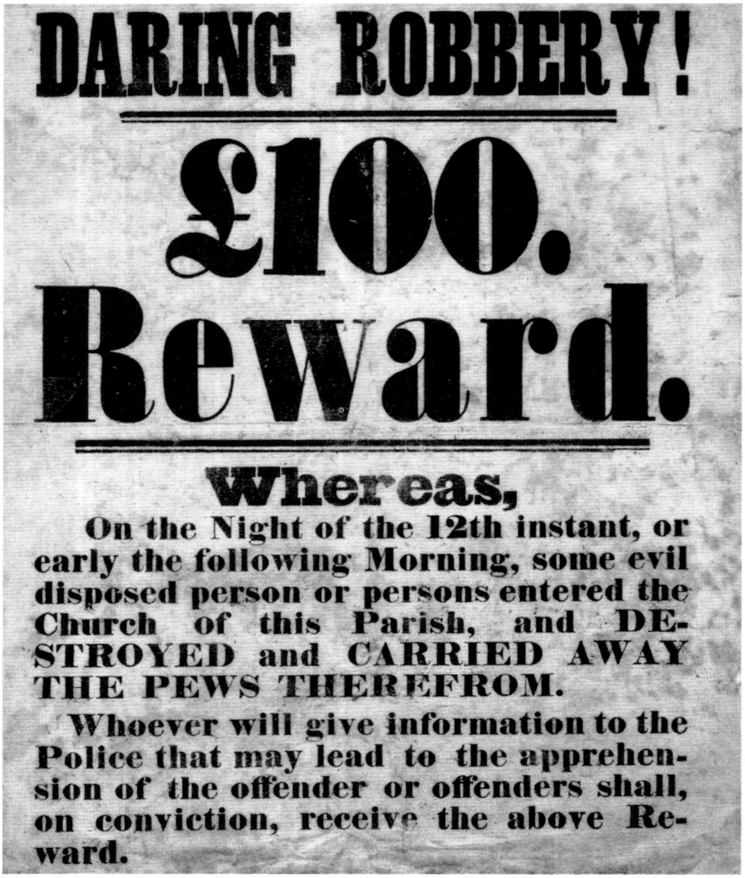

DARING ROBBERY!

£100. Reward.

Whereas,

On the Night of the 12th instant, or early the following Morning, some evil disposed person or persons entered the Church of this Parish, and DESTROYED and CARRIED AWAY THE PEWS THEREFROM.

Whoever will give information to the Police that may lead to the apprehension of the offender or offenders shall, on conviction, receive the above Reward.

79. Poster of October 1852 offering £100 reward for the apprehension of the men who had destroyed the church pews.

needed by subscription. His Vicar's Warden, **David Waddington**, who was also chairman of the Eastern Counties Railway, hired a gang of workmen in Norwich and transported them to Enfield by special train under cover of darkness. The church door was left unlocked and by the following morning the old box pews were a pile of splintered wood in the churchyard and the workmen responsible were already on their way back to Norwich. From this time Heath's incumbency slid into chaos. A poll of the parish voters on the pew issue was broken up by a no-popery mob from Ponders End assisted by the local rowdies fuelled on free drink distributed by the vicar's enemies. Heath was burnt in effigy in the Market Square on Guy Fawkes Night. A petition was sent to Parliament accusing him of popery and the Bishop of London appointed a commission of enquiry to investigate affairs at Enfield. *(See ill. 142 showing the pews at the centre of the controversy.)*

In 1864 Heath left Enfield on the grounds of ill health, leaving the church in the hands of a curate, **William Maclagan**. He finally resigned as vicar in

1870 and he died in 1882 in retirement at Milland near Haselmere and was brought back to Enfield for burial. His, tombstone bears the most appropriate of texts: 'Lord now lettest thou thy servant depart in peace'.

80. William Henderson (middle row, left), Enfield's first Labour MP, with his father Arthur Henderson (centre).

William Henderson

William Henderson (1891-1984) was Labour MP for Enfield from 1923-4 and 1929-31). He was the younger son of Arthur Henderson, one of the best-loved figures in the early Labour Party, who served as Home Secretary (1924) and Foreign Secretary (1929-31). During his second term as Enfield's MP, Henderson served as a junior minister at the India Office. Returning to Parliament in 1945 as Lord Henderson of Westgate, he held junior ministerial posts in the Attlee government, rising to Under Secretary of State at the Foreign Office 1950-1. (His counterpart in the Commons was Ernest Davies, the then MP for Enfield. Owing to the illness and death of the then Foreign

Secretary, Ernest Bevin, much of the work of the Foreign Office fell upon Henderson and Davies.) Like many sons of famous fathers, Henderson failed to live up to his promise.

Hertford Road

Literally the road to Hertford, it was also known as Ware Road, Waltham Road and the High Road, but not officially called Hertford Road until 1910. Before then it was designated in its various parts as Enfield Highway, Enfield Wash and Freezywater. The street numbering has been altered more than once and is a potential trap for unwary family history researchers. Between 1713 and 1826 it was under the control of the Stamford Hill and Green Lanes Turnpike Trust.

High Street

The southern continuation of Hertford Road running through Ponders End to the Edmonton border. It was sometimes known as Edmonton Road. Like Hertford Road, it was formerly under the control of the Stamford Hill and Green Lanes Turnpike Trust.

82. High Street, Ponders End, looking north towards Southbury Road.

George Hewitt Hodson

Hodson (1817-1904) was vicar of St Andrew's Church, Enfield from 1870 until his death. He was born at Edgbaston, the son of George Hodson, an Anglican clergyman, who later became Archdeacon of Stafford and a Canon of Lichfield Cathedral. After education at Trinity College, Cambridge and ordination Hodson worked as a curate in the Oxford suburbs, becoming vicar of Cookham Dean in Berkshire, before moving to Enfield. A staunch evangelical, Hodson's incumbency was marked by a virulent hatred of nonconformists and a deep dislike of school boards,

81. Hertford Road, Enfield Wash, looking north towards the Woolpack Bridge.

83. George Hodson, vicar of Enfield 1870-1904. He was the scourge of nonconformists and school boards.

which he saw as a threat to his Church schools. In order to stave off the threat of a School Board in Enfield, Hodson managed to conceal a shortage of school places by supplying the Board of Education with statistics which he must have known were inaccurate. In 1894 the Board of Education finally lost patience and ordered the setting up of a School Board in Enfield, but Hodson did not give up even then, getting himself elected onto the Board and trying unsuccessfully to wreck it from within.

Hodson's brother, William Hodson, an Indian Army Major, was responsible for one of the worst atrocities in the suppression of the Indian Mutiny, namely the shooting of several of the Mogul princes after the siege of Delhi in 1857. This was controversial even at the time. William Hodson was killed at Lucknow in 1858. George Hodson was fiercely protective of his brother's reputation, writing a book, *Hodson of Hodson's Horse*, based on his brother's letters and diaries.

In 1873, in conjunction with **Edward Ford**, he wrote *A History of Enfield*, contributing all the material on Church history. His work is still useful today, but, in view of his known biases, needs to be read with a degree of caution.

Hoe Lane

Called Hoo Lane in 1572, the name had assumed its modern form by 1754.The eastern end was sometimes called Magpie Lane after a former pub.

Holtwhites Hill

This was a trackway across The Chase linking Parsonage Lane and Chase Side with Lavender Hill. At the time of enclosure (1803) it was known as Parsonage Lane Road, but it appears on the 1867 Ordnance Survey under its modern name. Thomas Holt White, nephew of the naturalist, Gilbert White, lived at Chase Lodge, which stood on the south side of the road and was later demolished to make way for the railway. He died in 1841 and was buried in the churchyard at Harlow, Essex, where the memorial can still be seen.

Sir Frederick Gowland Hopkins

One of the leading biochemists of his generation, Hopkins (1861-1947) was born at Eastbourne, related through his father to the poet, Gerard Manley Hopkins. After his father's death, he and his mother moved to Enfield, settling at Lilburn Lodge, a house at the junction of The Ridgeway and Uplands Park Road close to his uncle, James Gowland. He studied medicine at Guy's Hospital, doing much of his reading on the train between Enfield and Liverpool Street. The high

84. Chase Lodge, Holtwhites Hill, the home of Thomas Holt White. It was demolished to make way for the Great Northern Railway's Cuffley extension.

point of his career came in 1929, when he won the Nobel Prize for the discovery of vitamins. One of his daughters, Jacquetta, was married first to the archaeologist, Christopher Hawkes, and subsequently to the novelist and dramatist, J B Priestley. She was a prolific writer on archaeology and related subjects under the name of Jacquetta Hawkes.

Hospitals

The hospitals serving the Enfield area are of widely differing origins and only came under common management on the formation of the National Health Service in 1948. Two, Chase Farm and the North Middlesex, are based in former Poor Law premises and were once local authority hospitals under the control of the old Middlesex County Council, as was the former St. Michael's Hospital. The War Memorial Hospital was a voluntary hospital and Highlands and South Lodge both began as isolation hospitals.

Chase Farm, The Ridgeway

The building was erected in 1886 by the Edmonton Board of Guardians as a Poor Law orphanage, the Chase Farm School. Control passed to Mid-

85. Chase Farm Hospital, built in 1886 as Chase Farm School.

86. The children's ward at the former Highlands Hospital.

dlesex County Council in 1930 and within a short time the children were dispersed to smaller children's homes elsewhere. After being used briefly to house old people, the building became a hospital in 1939. During the last war it was used to deal with air raid casualties from a large sector of North London. Since 1948 the hospital has been enlarged and refurbished, but plans for a new general hospital on the site were dropped in 1990 ostensibly on the grounds of cost. Since then Chase Farm has found itself merged with Barnet General Hospital for reasons that had less to do with efficiency than the huge debts run up by the latter when it was run by the notoriously incompetent Well House Trust (known to *Private Eye* readers as the 'Shit House Trust'). Proposals to concentrate accident and emergency services at Barnet, thereby sentencing Chase Farm to a lingering death, provoked a huge outcry in Enfield in 2005. Two years later, the battle continues. The very idea of concentrating A&E services at Barnet shows an ignorance of local geography and public transport routes, and suggests a level of crassness unusual even by the low standards of most NHS management. In the meantime property developers continue to show an unhealthy interest in the Chase Farm site.

Highlands, Worlds End Lane

This was built in 1884 by the Metropolitan Asylums Board as the Northern Isolation Hospital, its patients mainly being drawn from inner London. In 1930 control passed to the London County Council, and in 1939 it became an emergency bed service hospital and as such provided care for many wartime air raid casualties. Highlands became a general hospital after 1948, but it was an unsuitable building since, as it was built as an isolation unit, it had buildings scattered around a very large site. In 1966 it took over the adjoining South Lodge Hospital.

During the 1990s Highlands was gradually closed and the site sold off for housing, a process largely complete by 1997. A few token hospital buildings have been refurbished and converted into flats, but apart from this, the main link with the past has been the naming of new streets after prominent medical men. The new development, called Highlands Village, the name clearly intended to evoke an entirely bogus idyllic rural past, is irredeemably dull. To

87. The former South Lodge Hospital, opened 1900 as the Enfield Isolation Hospital.

pacify protestors, a new building at Chase Farm was named the Highlands Wing.

North Middlesex, Sterling Way
This was built in 1842 by the Edmonton Board of Guardians as the Edmonton Union Workhouse, which from the very beginning had some medical facilities. In 1910 a separate infirmary block was built. In 1915 the building was taken over by the War Office as the Edmonton Military Hospital and on its return to civilian use in 1920 it became the North Middlesex Hospital. An outpatients department opened in 1922, followed in 1930 by a radium department for treating cancers.

In 1930 control passed to Middlesex County Council, which drew up plans for a complete rebuilding, but these were thwarted by the outbreak of war. The building sustained some bomb damage, particularly in 1944. (An aunt of the author was in the hospital at the time giving birth to her one and only son.)

Since 1948 the hospital has been progressively rebuilt and at the time of writing the most substantial remnant of the former workhouse is the 1910 infirmary block. It is currently known as the North Middlesex University Hospital, reflecting an enhanced role in training doctors and nurses and a link with Middlesex University.

88. The War Memorial Hospital, opened 1875 as Enfield Cottage Hospital.

St Michael's, Chase Side Crescent
This was housed in the old Enfield workhouse, built in 1827. When Middlesex County Council took over in 1930, it became a public assistance institution known as Enfield House and was used to house the elderly and infirm, but after 1948 it became a geriatric hospital known as St Michael's. The building was demolished in 1997 with most of the site sold for housing. At the time of writing the NHS retains a small part of the site, the Magnolia Unit, used to provide respite care for the chronically sick.

South Lodge, Worlds End Lane
This was opened in 1900 by Enfield Urban District Council as the Enfield Isolation Hospital replacing a temporary corrugated iron building that had been erected in Lincoln Road in 1891. It was something of a triumph for Enfield's medical officer of health, **Dr John James Ridge**, who had been pressing for an isolation hospital ever since his appointment in 1881. Edmonton Council subsequently took a half share in the hospital and from 1905 it was run by the Enfield and Edmonton Joint Hospital Board. After 1948 it became a general hospital and was renamed South Lodge (after a former lodge on Enfield Chase). In 1966 it was merged with the adjoining Highlands Hospital and together with the rest of the Highlands site has since been closed and redeveloped for housing.

War Memorial, Chase Side
This voluntary institution opened in 1875 as the Enfield Cottage Hospital. The prime movers were **Dr John James Ridge** and James Whatman Bosanquet, a wealthy banker of Huguenot extraction, who lived at Clayesmore, Clay Hill. (Bosanquet's bank subsequently merged with Lloyds.) The building was enlarged as and when finance permitted – an operating theatre and a new ward in 1897/8 and a children's ward in 1906. (The author sampled the delights of the latter at the age of six in 1955, when he had his tonsils removed. He recalls a particu-

89. Christmas Day at the War Memorial Hospital with Dr Howard Distin carving the turkey. Hopefully, he was as skilful when operating on patients.

larly unpleasant night nurse, whose reign of terror ended, when she slipped on a highly polished floor while carrying a bowl of water, much to the amusement of the children.) In 1920 it was renamed the War Memorial Hospital and a substantial new wing was completed in 1926. The building was sold for redevelopment in 1984 and the site is now occupied by a sheltered housing complex called Borrowdale Court

Huguenots

Several Huguenot families settled in Enfield. The earliest was the Garnault family of Bulls Cross, long connected with the New River Company. They lived at Bowling Green House, which was later demolished to make way for **Myddelton House**, and were intermarried with the Romilly family. Daniel Garnault died in 1809 and the property passed to his sister Anne, wife of Henry Carrington Bowles, a wealthy publisher and print seller. From them are descended the Bowles and Parker Bowles families.

James Whatman Bosanquet was a wealthy banker, whose ancestors had lived at Montpelier. He bought Clayesmore (off Clay Hill) in 1847 and lived here until his death. His brother Captain (later Admiral) Bosanquet lived nearby at Wildwoods. Other branches of the family lived at Walthamstow, Broxbourne and Southgate.

James Rondeau, a member of a family long settled at Spitalfields, ran a private school at Clay Hill, but by 1826 had moved to the Manor House, Bulls Cross.

Industry

Of Enfield's traditional industries the most remarkable survivor is Ponders End Mill, now powered by electricity rather than by the water of the Lee. Some of its buildings date back to the 18th century and it is likely that there has been a mill on this site since the Normans. The business has been in the hands of the Wright family for well over a hundred years. Brickmaking is now finally extinct in Enfield and gravel digging has left behind a scabrous

90. The foundry at United Flexible Metal Tubing, Scotland Green, c.1910.

and poisonous legacy. The once ubiquitous market garden industry has been reduced to a few remnants in the Crews Hill area supplying the local garden centres.

Enfield's industrial base has suffered a near total collapse over the last 20 years. Of the once mighty Royal Small Arms Factory (1816-1988) a few remnants remain in a somewhat lifeless housing development euphemistically named Enfield Island Village. Once famous companies such as Belling, Belling-Lee, Thorn and United Flexible Metal Tubing have either left Enfield or, in most cases, sunk from memory. The Great Cambridge Road has seen its factories succumb one by one to be replaced by retail developments redolent of a crudely resurgent commercialism.

Hugh Jenkins

Hugh Jenkins (1908-94) was a prominent Labour politician. He was born in Lancaster Road, Enfield in a flat over a dairy run by his Welsh-born father, Joseph Jenkins and his mother was a member of the Gater family which ran a butcher's shop nearby in Chase Side. The Jenkins family later moved to Gordon Hill.

Jenkins was educated locally at Chase Side School and Enfield Grammar School. He was an active trade unionist, becoming deputy general secretary of Equity, the actor's union. In 1950 he unsuccessfully contested Enfield West for the Labour Party against **Iain Macleod** but eventually reached the Commons in 1964 when he won Putney, hitherto regarded as a safe Conservative seat. He served as Arts Minister (1974-76) in Harold Wilson's second government, a lively, colourful and controversial figure. Defeated at Putney in 1979, by David Mellor, he later went to the Lords as Lord Jenkins of Putney. In his old age he wrote *Solo Boy*, a play performed on BBC Radio 4, based on his experiences as a choirboy at Christ Church Congregational Church in Chase Side. One of his contemporaries at Enfield Grammar School was the travel writer **Norman Lewis**, also the son of a Welsh father.

Jews

Enfield, unlike its neighbours Tottenham and Southgate, has never had a particularly large Jewish population. However, there was a small Jewish presence from the late 18th century onwards.

Hanamel D'Aguila, a member of a prolific Sephardi family, is listed in a rate book of 1794 living close to the junction of Hertford Road and Turkey Street. (His home was almost certainly Grove House, later the residence of Matthew Michell, patron of the artist, Thomas Rowlandson.)

Benjamin D'Israeli (father of Isaac and grandfather of the Prime Minister) lived at Baker Street (probably Carlton House) from 1782. In 1802 Benjamin Mendes Da Costa, a member of a Sephardi family long resident at Highgate, lived at Enfield Highway when he was married (out of the faith) at St Andrew's Church, to Louise Naylor, the daughter of a wealthy Ponders End coal merchant. (A son of this marriage settled in Australia, where he founded one of the country's first public schools.)

The 1851 census lists a Jewish family living at the Manor House, Bulls Cross. Aaron Da Costa was a merchant, aged 49 and born at Hackney. Living with him were his wife and six children, two of whom had been born in Jamaica.

By the late 19th century a small number of Jewish business men had established themselves in Enfield. A directory of 1899 lists three Jewish tailors – David Goldberg at Enfield Highway, A. Lazarus at Enfield Lock and Philip Kronman at Enfield Wash.

By the end of the last war a number of Jewish families had settled in and around Enfield Town, including several on the Willow Estate. To cater for their needs the Enfield and Winchmore Hill Synagogue was set up in a converted house in Wellington Road, Bush Hill Park. (Immediately before the war the house had been used as a staging post for Jewish children brought out of Germany and Austria by the Kindertransport.)

Sir Frederic Wood Jones

Jones (1879-1954) was one of the leading anatomists of his generation. He was born in Hackney, but when he was still a child, the family moved to Enfield, settling in Private Road, Bush Hill Park. He was educated at Enfield Grammar School, subsequently studying medicine at the London Hospital.

Boris Karloff

Karloff (1887-1969) was born William Henry Pratt at Dulwich, the family later moving to Enfield. At the time of the 1901 census the family was living at Norgrove, a large house still standing in Uplands Park Road. (The author's grandfather, who lived nearby on The Ridgeway, remembered having a fight with the future film star.) He went on the stage under the name of Boris Karloff, later emigrating to the USA, where he had a long and successful career as a film and stage actor. He is particularly remembered for his work in some of the early horror films.

John Keats

Keats (1795-1821) was the son of a wealthy publican in the City of London and was educated at John Clarke's school (on the site of Enfield Town Station) where he was befriended by the proprietor's son, **Charles Cowden Clarke**. Sadly, both his parents died young, his father from injuries sustained in a riding accident and his mother from what was probably tuberculosis. On leaving school he took up medicine and served as an apprentice to Edmonton doctor, Thomas Hammond of Church Street. He subsequently enrolled as a medical student at Guy's Hospital. At this time he was already writing poetry and he made the momentous decision to give up medicine to become a full-time writer. Just as he was beginning to acquire a reputation as a poet, he was diagnosed with tuberculosis, a disease which had already carried off his mother, an uncle and one of his brothers. He travelled to Italy in the hope that he might recover his health, but died in Rome.

Legh Kilpin

Kilpin (1853-1919) was born in the Isle of Wight and later trained at the National Art Training School at South Kensington. Between 1880 and 1902 he taught art at Enfield Grammar School. He subsequently emigrated to Canada, where he taught at the Montreal Technical Institute and elsewhere. He was an accomplished painter in both oil and watercolour and also did etchings and engravings. A major retrospective exhibition was staged in Canada in 2003.

91. *John Keats, painting by Joseph Severn, 1821.*

93. *Charles Lamb, from a painting by Garrick.*

Charles Lamb

Lamb's essays are widely regarded as a benchmark of the English language. He grew up in the Fleet Street area of London and worked for many years for the East India Company. After his retirement, Lamb (1775-1834) and his sister Mary (1764-1847), moved to Enfield from their home at Colebrook Row, Islington. (The couple had previously visited Enfield, staying at Clarendon Cottage, Gentleman's Row.) Their first permanent home in Enfield was at The Poplars, Chase Side, but the strain of running the home proved to be too much for Mary and they later moved next door as lodgers in the house of Thomas Westwood (now called Westwood Cottage). Mary suffered a series of mental breakdowns - indeed, at Colebrook Row in 1796, in a fit of rage at a servant girl she had inadvertently fatally stabbed her mother. Her condition deteriorated even further as she grew older, and it was this that caused them to again move in 1833 to Edmonton, where appropriate medical attention was more readily available.

92. *Westwood Cottage (left) and The Poplars, both occupied at different times by Charles Lamb and his sister, Mary.*

They settled at Bay Cottage, Church Street and it was here that Charles died. He (and later Mary) were buried nearby in All Saints churchyard, where their grave can still be seen. Throughout his time in Enfield Lamb kept up a correspondence with a wide circle of friends. His letters provide a lively, humorous and occasionally malicious commentary on people and events and much about the state of Enfield at the time.

94. A group of shops on the north side of Lancaster Road.

Lancaster Road

Originally known as New Lane, but by the time the area began to develop the name was deemed inappropriate. In 1887 the Enfield Local Board renamed it Lancaster Road after Enfield's onetime manorial landlord, the Duchy of Lancaster.

Lavender Hill

A former trackway across The Chase linking New Lane (Lancaster Road) with Holtwhites Hill and The Ridgeway, it was known as New Lane Road in 1803. By 1850 it was Lavender Hill – an adjoining area, used for cultivating lavender, was known as the Lavender Fields.

Lea Valley Road

This road was built by public subscription in 1873 to link Ponders End and Chingford. Before, there was just a footpath across the marshes from Ponders End to Sewardstone Road. Originally connected with South Street, the road was diverted in 1964 to link up with Nag's Head Road, thereby enabling the level crossing at Ponders End Station to be closed and through traffic moved away from South Street.

The Lee Navigation

The River Lee in its natural state was more or less navigable as far upstream as Ware and Hertford. In 894 a force of invading Danes sailed from the North Sea into the Thames estuary and then up the Lee to a point about twenty miles north of London probably close to Ware. The opposing Saxon forces under the command of Alfred responded by building two forts on either side of the river and placing obstructions in the river bed; the Danes were forced to abandon their boats and escaped overland into Essex.

In medieval times a substantial proportion of London's grain supply was carried down the Lee. The river bed had many shoals and sandbanks and in summer months, when the water level dropped, navigation became especially difficult. There were frequent disputes (some violent) between millers and bargemen, both of whose livelihoods were dependent on the water.

In 1190 the Abbot of Waltham straightened a section of the river at Waltham Abbey and in 1425 an Act of Parliament appointed commissioners to deal with obstructions in the river bed and generally to improve navigation between London and Hertford.

In 1571 another Act was passed to improve navigation between London and Ware. As a result sections of the river were extensively scoured and embanked and at Waltham Abbey a lock, one of the very earliest pound locks in the country, was installed by 1577. The improvements encouraged an extensive trade in malt between Ware and London, moving from road to river, thus threatening the livelihoods of the Enfield maltmen who had previously dominated the business. Their response was violent. Matters came to a head in 1581 when saboteurs cut the banks of the river near Green Street and there was an attempt to burn the new lock at Waltham.

In 1738 trustees were appointed to superintend the navigation. The River Lee Act of 1766 authorised the building of new locks and lock cuts and the construction of a new outlet to the Thames – the

95. One of the last barge horses on the Lee Navigation, pictured at Waltham Lock.

96. Ponders End Lock in 1955.

Limehouse Cut. The work was supervised by John Smeaton.

In 1769 the River Stort navigation was opened from the Lee at Rye House to Bishop's Stortford. Plans (ultimately abortive) were prepared for a canal linking the Stort with the River Cam. (Had this been built, there would be a continuous line of inland waterway linking London with Cambridge, Ely and Kings Lynn.)

In 1830 the Hertford Union Canal opened between the Lee at Hackney and the Regent's Canal, providing a useful link with the Grand Union Canal at Paddington. An Act of 1855 authorised a new lock at Amwell Marsh, the rebuilding of Picketts Lock and the removal of Stanstead and Edmonton Locks. In 1869 the newly formed Lee Conservancy Board took over control from the former trustees.

In 1922-23 the locks between Enfield and Hertford were all rebuilt and enlarged. In 1948 along with other inland waterways the Lee was nationalised and placed under the control of the British Transport Commission, later passing to the British Waterways Board.

Cargoes downstream consisted predominantly of malt and grain destined for London, but the river also carried gunpowder from Waltham Abbey and rifles en route from the Royal Small Arms Factory to the Tower of London Armoury. Cargoes upstream included coal, timber and what was euphemistically described as London manure.

Today, commercial traffic is largely confined to the lower reaches of the Lee. Above Enfield the river is mostly given over to pleasure craft.

Norman Lewis

A travel writer of international reputation, Lewis (1908-2003) was born in Enfield, the son of Richard Lewis, a Welsh-born pharmacist, who had a shop in Lancaster Road, later moving to Southbury Road. The family lived first in Sydney Road, but later were in a house in Carterhatch Lane that still stands close to the junction with Bridgenhall Road. Richard Lewis dabbled in spiritualism and was to establish the Beacon of Light Spiritualist Church that still survives in Carterhatch Lane. Norman, a delicate child, spent part of his childhood with his father's family in South Wales. Returning to Enfield, he was educated at Forty Hill School before winning a place at Enfield Grammar . One of his contemporaries there was the future Labour politician, **Hugh Jenkins**.

Lewis established himself as a travel writer of high quality, producing memorable books about Spain, Italy, Sicily and Indo-China. He was later to publicise the plight of the native population of the Amazon rain forest in an important article for the *Sunday Times.* In 1985 he produced an at times wickedly funny autobiography, *Jackdaw Cake,* in which he recalled his childhood in Enfield. He had great fun at the expense of the once locally powerful Bowles family, mischievously drawing attention to the marital infidelities of **Sir Henry Bowles** and daring to suggest that his brother, **Gussie Bowles**, was a homosexual. Locally, this sparked a virulently hostile reaction from elements within Enfield, who did not like to see their idols knocked off their plinths. Lewis was undeterred and wrote an even funnier sequel, *God Bless the Squire,* published in *The Happy Ant Heap* (1998). Lewis' final work, *A Tomb in Seville,* in which he recalled events in Spain as the Civil War broke out in 1936, was published a few months after his death.

97. The Enfield Central Library in Cecil Road, opened in 1912.

Libraries

The 1850 Public Libraries Act gave local authorities the powers to set up public libraries, but limited expenditure to a rate of one halfpenny in the pound. A later Act (1855) raised this to one penny in the pound - the rate restriction was finally lifted altogether in 1919, when library powers were extended to county councils.

The public library movement was slow to take root in the London area and particularly slow in outer London - this was due to the chaotic state of London local government rather than any lack of need.

The Enfield Local Board adopted the Public Libraries Act in 1892 one year after Edmonton. In 1894 a temporary library opened, housed in one room of the Public Offices in Gentleman's Row (now the Registry Office). Permanent buildings followed after financial assistance from the Carnegie Trust. The Enfield Highway Library in Hertford Road opened in 1910, followed in 1912 by the Central Library in Cecil Road. Further expansion had to wait until after the last war.

In 1948 the Bush Hill Park Library in Fourth Avenue opened in a building previously used by St Mark's School. The same year saw the introduction of a mobile library to serve outlying areas and the beginning of a pioneering gramophone record library at the Central Library. New branch libraries opened at Kempe Road (1957), Ponders End (1962) and Enfield Road (1964). The Central Library was refurbished and extended with a new children's library and an enlarged lending library.

In April 1965 the newly formed London Borough of Enfield took over the Edmonton and Enfield library systems plus the Southgate section of Middlesex County Libraries. A new branch in Southgate High Street (inherited from Middlesex County Libraries) opened in 1966, but other schemes were less successful. Plans for libraries at Hadley Wood and Angel Road, Edmonton ultimately came to nothing. A substantial new building in Ordnance Road displaced in 1976 the Enfield Highway Library as the principal library in East Enfield. Since then, persistent

98. Enfield Highway Library, Hertford Road, opened in 1910.

99. An early view of the Central Library's lending department. The library then worked on a closed access system with readers choosing books using the cards on the indicator board (right).

financial problems have resulted in a dramatic slowing of progress and an increasing reliance upon converted buildings.

A new Weir Hall Library replaced the previous building demolished for road widening in 1988 on a site in Silver Street, Edmonton, which it shared with the impecunious Millfield Theatre. In 1991 the original Edmonton Library of 1897, by this time a listed building, was abandoned and subsequently sold, the service moving to a refurbished Co-op shop in Edmonton Green Shopping Centre. The branch in Houndsfield Road was closed at the same time. In 1992 the former De Bohun Library in Green Road, another listed building, was closed and the building sold. In 2006 a new Oakwood Library opened in another former Co-op shop in Bramley Road, enabling the Merryhills Library in Enfield Road to be closed and sold for redevelopment.

Charles Lightoller

Lightoller (1874-1952) was born at Chorley, Lancashire and went to sea at the age of fourteen in 1888, joining the White Star Line in 1900. In April 1912, as 2nd Officer of the *Titanic*, he was the most senior of the ship's officers to survive the sinking and was a key witness at the enquiries held subsequently in Washington and London. During the First World War he served with distinction in the RNVR. Returning to the White Star Line after the war, he served as Chief officer of the *Celtic*, but soon discovered that further promotion was blocked by his association with the *Titanic* disaster and he eventually resigned. In 1932 he and his family settled at The Cottage, Games Road, Cockfosters, where he successfully ran a poultry farm. In 1940, at the age of sixty-six, he came out of retirement to take part in the Dunkirk evacuation. Two of his sons were killed in the last war. In 1946 he moved to Twickenham to assist his remaining son, Roger, in running a boatyard.

Lincoln Road

Prior to the upgrading of Nag's Head Lane (Southbury Road) at the time of enclosure, Lincoln Road was the principal link between Enfield Town and Ponders End. The pronounced bend immediately east of the A10 marks the spot where Roman **Ermine Street** once crossed. This road has had more names than any other Enfield street. It has been known as Ayley Croft Lane, Brick Kiln Lane, Brickfield Lane, Bungey Lane, Red Lane and Joan Potter's Lane. The present name dates only from 1870 and was initially applied to a short stretch at the eastern end, developed as part of the Lincoln House Estate. The whole road was officially renamed Lincoln Road by the Enfield Local Board of Health in 1888. Today, through traffic is seriously impeded by a railway level crossing which is closed to road traffic evenings and weekends.

100. An early 20th-century view of Lincoln Road looking towards the railway from London Road.

Local Government

In the post medieval period the principal unit of local government was the Vestry. This originated as an annual meeting of prominent parishioners in the church vestry room, normally held at Easter, to elect the churchwardens for the coming year. During the Tudor period an increasing number of civil functions, such as poor relief and highway maintenance, became parish responsibilities and the vestries, once exclusively concerned with church affairs, gradually took on a local government function.

The 1834 Poor Law Amendment Act took away the vestries' Poor Law powers and put them in the hands of new directly elected authorities, the Poor Law unions, run by boards of guardians - locally, the Edmonton Board of Guardians provided for the poor of Hornsey, Tottenham, Edmonton, Enfield, Cheshunt, Waltham Abbey and, for a short time only, Hampstead.

In 1850 Enfield Vestry lost its remaining local government powers to the Enfield Local Board of Health, a directly elected body set up under the terms of the 1848 Public Health Act. (Edmonton and Tottenham also had local boards of health.) This body later gave way to the Enfield Urban District Council established under the 1894 Local Government Act.

Education was provided by private enterprise and the voluntary (usually religious) sector, but during the 19th century, with massive population growth in urban areas, government intervention became inevitable and the 1870 Education Act was passed giving powers for the establishment of directly elected school boards in districts where there was a deficiency of school places, but the Enfield School Board was not set up until 1894. The 1902 Education Act abolished school boards and established local authority education committees. Enfield Education Committee took over from the School Board in 1903

The 1888 Local Government Act had provision for the establishment of county councils - local government at county level had previously been carried out by the county justices meeting at quarter sessions. Middlesex County Council was set up in 1889, but at the same time much of the inner part of the county (Stepney, Hackney, Westminster, Kensington, etc.) was placed under the control of the newly formed London County Council.

In the 1930s there were discussions as to whether Enfield should seek borough status. However, squabbles over ward boundaries and then the outbreak of war prevented progress.(In the meantime, Southgate had become a borough in 1933, followed by Edmonton in 1937.) In the post-war period the idea was revived and on 23rd May 1955 Enfield finally became a municipal borough, when a charter of incorporation was presented by the then Lord

101. The final meeting of the former Enfield Borough Council in March 1965.

Mayor of London, Sir Seymour Howard.

Enfield's life as a borough was to be short. In 1960 a Royal Commission on London Government recommended some drastic changes. Both the London County Council and Middlesex Council were to be abolished in favour of a Greater London Council and large chunks of suburban Surrey, Kent and Essex, plus a small portion of Hertfordshire, were to be brought into this new county. At district level, councils were to be merged into larger units – the new London boroughs, and under the 1963 London Government Act, implemented in 1965, Enfield was merged with Edmonton and Southgate to form the London Borough of Enfield. At the same time, Middlesex County Council was abolished. The new borough took on enhanced powers, especially in the fields of education and social services, which had previously been run at county level.

In 1974 some health services, such as baby clinics, were placed under the control of the newly formed health authorities. In 1986 the Greater London Council, having managed to seriously alienate Margaret Thatcher's Conservative government, was abolished and its functions distributed among the London boroughs and an array of joint committees. However, in the longer term this move was widely perceived to have been a mistake and in 2000 a London-wide authority, the Greater London Assembly, was set up, with a directly elected mayor.

Local Newspapers

The *Enfield Gazette* was first published in 1859 as the *Enfield Observer*. It was founded by John Henry Meyers, a printer in Enfield Town. In its early days so little was happening in Enfield that the paper was published only monthly. A short-lived rival, the *Enfield Chronicle* appeared in 1898 and survived until 1903. A more formidable rival was the *Enfield Weekly Herald*, an offshoot of the long-established *Tottenham & Edmonton Weekly Herald*. This was published from 1921 until the closure of the Herald Group in 1983. In more recent years free sheets have entered the field: the *Enfield Independent*, the *Enfield Advertiser* (now owned by the same company as the *Gazette*) and the short-lived *Enfield Post*.

REGISTERED FOR | MEYERS' | TRANSMISSION ABROAD.

ENFIELD OBSERVER

AND LOCAL ADVERTISER:

A Monthly Record for Enfield and the surrounding Parishes.

No. 13, NEW SERIES | JANUARY 1st, 1860. | [PRICE 1½d., with Extra Number 3d.

TWO SERMONS
Will be preached, (D.V.) in
THE OLD INDEPENDENT CHAPEL
CHASE SIDE, ENFIELD.
On SUNDAY, JANUARY 1st, 1860,
BY THE
Rev. JOHN STRIBLING.
Subject of the Morning Discourse —
The Blessing pronounced by Moses upon the Tribe of Asher.
That of the Evening —
Joshua's Charge to the Children of Israel.

The Ordinance of the Lord's Supper will be administered after the Morning service.

To be followed on succeeding Sundays by a course of Sermons on various important subjects, which will be duly announced.

Divine Service commences in the Morning at ½-past 10, and in the Evening at ½-past 6 o'Clock.

A Weekly Service every Thursday Evening at

J. H. MEYERS,
PRINTER, PUBLISHER,
Bookseller and Stationer,
PUBLIC LIBRARY, ENFIELD.

BOOKBINDING IN ALL ITS BRANCHES.
MS. MUSIC BOOKS 1s. EACH.
PRESENT BOOKS IN HANDSOME BINDINGS.

PLAIN & FANCY STATIONERY
ENVELOPES 5s. per 1000.
ALMANACS, DIARIES, and POCKET BOOKS
FOR MDCCCLX.

For the purpose of clearing off the whole of the remaining Stock of the Christmas Trees
A DRAW
Will take place on Wednesday, the 4th of January and following days. Tickets 6d. and 1s. each, to be had at the Public Library.

TESTAMENTS and PRAYER BOOKS,

R. C. DRUMMOND,
RAILWAY HOTEL,
ADJOINING THE STATION.

R. C. D. Respectfully thanks his patrons and their friends for the large amount of support he has received, and to inform them that he is enabled from his connexions with the London trade, at this time of the year, to offer a reduction in the spirit trade. He begs to call their attention to the following List of Prices :—

WINES—Crusted Port 4s. per bottle, 48s. per dozen ; ditto 4s. 6d. per bottle, 54s. per dozen. Fine Nutty flavoured Sherry 4s. per bottle, 48s. per dozen ; Amontalado ditto 4s. 6d. per bottle, 54s. per dozen. Wine in pints—Port 3s., Claret 2s. 6d. per pint.

(The Spirits are from the firm of Sir Robert Burnett & Co., of Vauxhall, allowed by all in the trade to be the best on town.)

BRANDY—Very old and of delicate flavour 4s. 6d. per bottle, 28s. per gallon ; fine Champagne ditto 5s. and 5s. 6d. per bottle, 33s. per gallon.

102. The front page of the Enfield Observer, *1 January 1860.*

103. London Road looking north towards The Town. The road was later widened for the tramway.

London Road

The principal approach to Enfield Town from the south, known variously as London Way and London Lane, acquired its present name by 1871. Like Hertford Road, it was formerly under the control of the Stamford Hill and Green Lanes Turnpike Trust. The road was widened in 1909 to make room for tram tracks.

Sir Thomas Lovell

Lovell (*c*.1450-1524) was Chancellor of the Exchequer to both Henry VII and Henry VIII. He first entered Parliament in 1485 and served briefly as Speaker of The Commons before becoming Chancellor, a post he held without a break until 1516. He came from a legal background and was active in the affairs of Lincoln's Inn, serving both as governor and treasurer. (A Tudor gatehouse at Lincoln's Inn still bears Lovell's Arms.)

Lovell was by birth an East Anglian, coming from the Norfolk village of East Harling. In 1508 he inherited Elsing, a substantial house (now demolished), which stood on the meadow between Forty Hall and Maidens Brook. It was here that Lovell died in 1524. He was buried at Holywell Priory, Shoreditch – the tomb was destroyed when the priory was dissolved and subsequently demolished. Lovell had no children and Elsing was inherited by Thomas Manners, Earl of Rutland, who was related to Lovell's second wife. Lovell's badge (a wing) can still be seen in the clerestory of St. Andrew's Church.

M25

This motorway had its origins in Sir Charles Bressey's 1924 plan for a North Orbital Road from Staines to Tilbury via Watford, St Albans, Hoddesdon and Brentwood, with either a bridge or tunnel providing a link across the Thames at Dartford. It then appeared in a slightly revised form as the D Ring Road in Sir Patrick Abercrombie's *Greater London Plan* of 1944. It was finally completed in 1984. Enfield is served by the junction with the A10 north of Bullsmoor Lane and the junction at Potters Bar.

104. Construction work on the bridge carrying the M25 across Cattlegate Road.

105. John Mackie was MP for Enfield East 1959-74.

106. William Dalrymple Maclagan, curate-in-charge of St Andrew's church 1865-9. The photograph was taken when he was Bishop of Lichfield.

John Mackie

John Mackie (1909-95) was Labour MP for Enfield East from 1959 to 1974. He was by birth a Highland Scot and by profession a farmer, running for many years the Harold Park Farm at Nazeing, Essex. During the first Wilson administration (1964-70) Mackie served as a junior agriculture minister (1967-70). He retired from the Commons in February 1974, later going to the Lords as Lord John-Mackie. His brother, George Mackie, was Liberal MP for Caithness and Sutherland (1964-66).

William Dalrymple Maclagan

Maclagan (1826-1910) was born and grew up in Edinburgh. He worked briefly in a lawyer's office and then served in the Indian Army 1847-49, resigning on health grounds. Then after studying at Peterhouse, he was ordained in 1856 into the Church of England, and between 1865 and 1869 he was curate-in-charge of St Andrew's Church, Enfield Town in decidedly curious circumstances. The then Vicar, **John Moore Heath,** who had been in post since 1844, left Enfield pleading ill health, but remained vicar until resigning the living in 1870. Heath, an Anglo-Catholic in a parish overwhelmingly Evangelical in sympathy saw his incumbency degenerate into a series of running battles with his congregation, culminating in the memorable pew controversy of 1853-54. Maclagan inherited a deeply troubled and strife-riven parish, a situation that he handled with great skill and tact, and he did much to repair the damage done in Heath's time. He subsequently served as vicar of Newington, Southwark (1869-75) and of St Mary Abbots, Kensington (1875-78). He then became Bishop of Lichfield (1878-91) and Archbishop of York (1891-1908).

107. Iain Macleod was MP for Enfield West 1950-70.

Iain Macleod

Iain Macleod (1913-70) was Conservative MP for Enfield West from 1950 until his death. He was born at Skipton, Yorkshire, but both his parents were Scots from the Western Isles. Soon after his election at Enfield he attracted attention as a fine orator and a tough debater and within two years he was in the cabinet as Minister of Health. He subsequently served as Minister of Labour, Colonial Secretary, Leader of the House of Commons, and briefly as Conservative Party Chairman. As Colonial Secretary he was responsible for granting independence to large parts of the British Empire. In 1963 Macleod resigned from the Conservative front bench rather than serve under Sir Alec Douglas-Home, who had succeeded Harold Macmillan as Prime Minister.

He then worked for a time as editor of *The Spectator*. He returned to the Conservative front bench in 1965, by which time the party was in opposition. The Conservatives returned to office in June 1970 and Macleod was appointed Chancellor of the Exchequer in Edward Heath's government. But his triumph was shortlived. Returning home to no.11 Downing Street after an operation for appendicitis, he collapsed and died from a heart attack just short of his 57th birthday.

Macleod was small in stature and was slightly stooped as a result of the arthritis which seriously affected his neck, spine and shoulders, and in his later years he walked with the aid of a stick. He was a formidably good platform speaker – the author heard him address an election meeting in Enfield in 1970, possibly the last major public speech that he gave.

Arthur Heygate Mackmurdo

Mackmurdo (1851-1942) was born in Church Street, Edmonton, the son of Edward Mackmurdo, a long-serving churchwarden at All Saints Church. As a young man he got involved with William Morris' Arts and Crafts Movement and produced some fine work in fabric and wallpaper design and typography. In 1888 he founded the Century Guild to promote artistic craftsmanship, its journal, the *Hobby Horse*, being particularly influential. He also worked as an architect and in Enfield he built two adjoining houses in Private Road, Bush Hill Park – Halcyon House was built for his mother and Brooklyn (no.8) for his brother, Harold Mackmurdo. (Disgracefully, Halcyon House was allowed to be demolished in 1968, but Brooklyn has survived.) Mackmurdo's output as an architect was small but significant and he greatly influenced the work of another architect, Charles Voysey (1857-

108. Frederick Marryat, educated at the Rev. Stephen Freeman's Academy at Clay Hill.

1941). After 1904 he gave up all architectural and design work, spending the rest of his life promoting obscure social and political theories.

Frederick Marryat

Frederick Marryat (1792-1848) turned to writing full time after being forced by ill health to leave the Royal Navy. He was a prolific writer of sea stories such as the once widely read *Midshipman Easy,* but is now chiefly remembered for his perennially popular novel, *Children of the New Forest*.

He was educated in Enfield at the Rev. Stephen Freeman's Academy, located in a house called Holmwood, formerly standing at the junction with Baker Street and Clay Hill. (The site is marked by a blue plaque.) One of his contemporaries there was **Charles Babbage**.

William Mellish

William Mellish (1764-1838) came from a family long resident at Blyth, Nottinghamshire and inherited, through his mother, a large house that stood on the northern slopes of

109. William Mellish of Bush Hill Park.

Bush Hill. He became a director of the Bank of England and was Tory MP for Middlesex 1806-20. Mellish had previously been MP for Grimsby (1796-1802), a seat once held by his uncle, Joseph Mellish. His father, William Mellish senior had been MP for East Retford.

Mellish was a substantial landowner in both Enfield and Edmonton – most of modern Bush Hill Park was built over his land. There is a memorial tablet to him in All Saints, Edmonton. His brother, John Mellish of Hamels (now a golf club) near Braughing, died in 1798, reputedly the last man in England to be killed by a highwayman.

Methodism

The history of the Methodist Church is complicated by the fact that, after the death of the founder, John Wesley, the movement tended to fragment. In Enfield the two most important factions were the Wesleyan Methodists and the Primitive Methodists. (Happily, the differences were eventually resolved and the strands reunited in 1932)

In Enfield Town in 1845 Wesleyans held services in temporary premises in Baker Street, moving in 1864 to a new church in Cecil Road. In 1889 they moved again to their present building at the junction of Church Street and Little Park Gardens. This is now called Trinity Church and is now run jointly with the United Reformed Church, incorporating the congregation of the former St Paul's Presbyterian Church.

110. Trinity Church, built in 1889 by Wesleyan Methodists. It is now run jointly by the Methodists and the United Reformed Church.

In East Enfield, the Ponders End Methodist Church in the High Street (1931) traces its origins to a small chapel of 1849. The present church dates from 1857.

The Primitive Methodists were active in the Chase Side area and had built a chapel by 1858, moving to a larger building elsewhere in Chase Side in 1894. This became redundant after 1932 and was later used by the Salvation Army. There was also a Primitive Methodist Church in South Street, Ponders End. Just over the Edmonton border, the Bush Hill Park Methodist Church was founded by the Primitive Methodists in 1905.

Millmarsh Lane

Literally, the road linking Green Street to Mill Marsh, then used as grazing land. This later came to be one of Enfield's most heavily industrialised areas.

Myddelton House

This house was built in 1818 by Henry Carrington Bowles to replace Bowling Green House. He had acquired the property by his marriage to Anne, the heiress of the Garnault family. The house has a superb garden created by **E.A. 'Gussie' Bowles**, one of its features being the former Enfield market cross of 1826 *(ill. 112)*. The Bowles family connection ceased after the death of Gussie in 1954 and the house is now the head office of the Lee Valley Regional Park Authority.

Nag's Head Road

This road, built from 1890, assumed an important role in 1964 when it was extended eastwards, crossing the River Lee on a newly constructed viaduct, to link up with Lea Valley Road. This allowed the closure of the congested level crossing at Ponders End station and diversion of through traffic away from South Street.

111. A late 19th-century view of Myddelton House, home of the Bowles family.

The New River

It is neither new nor a river. In the early 17th century Sir Hugh Myddelton, a Welshman from Denbigh, devised a scheme to convey fresh water from Hertfordshire (springs at Ware and Amwell) into London. The New River Company was set up in 1606 with powers to construct a canal from Ware to the then northern outskirts of London at Clerkenwell, near the Angel, from where the water would be distributed to customers in the City. Construction was complete by1613.

The original course through Enfield differed considerably from that followed today. Entering Enfield from Cheshunt, the New River passes beneath Bullsmoor Lane and Turkey Street. At this point the original course veered away to the west, passing beneath Bulls Cross, where the site of the bridge can still be discerned. It then passed through the grounds of **Myddelton House** and the Whitewebbs Estate and crossed the Cuffley Brook close to Flash Lane, where the remains of an early 19th-century aqueduct can still be seen. The course then swung round to the opposite direction, running eastwards along the south side of the valley and crossed the Turkey Brook behind the club house of the Whitewebbs Golf Course, and passed through Gough Park, where it fed a small lake. There are substantial remains of this section, long stretches of which are still in water.(This area is best avoided on summer evenings, when mosquitoes are particularly voracious.) Emerging from Gough Park the River passed beneath Baker Street and crossed Ansell's Green, where its line (by this time dry) was still visible until obliterated by road works in 1971. It then traversed the Willow Estate roughly along the line of Eastbury Avenue and

112. The grounds of Myddelton House with the former Enfield Market Cross serving as a garden ornament. The garden was largely the creation of Gussie Bowles.

113. The New River Loop alongside the Town Park.

114. The New River Loop at Gentleman's Row. The site of Beauchamp Lodge (left) is now occupied by the houses in River View.

Carisbrooke Close to rejoin the present course at the eastern end of Tenniswood Road. (The present course between here and Turkey Street dates from 1859.) From here the River runs southwards to Southbury Road from where the water is now carried underground in cast iron pipes to rejoin the New River at Bush Hill. The old course running alongside Southbury Road, under Churchbury Lane and Silver Street, across Chase Green and the Town Park has been retained for ornamental purposes. (During the last war, after the cast iron pipes had been breeched by a bomb near Bush Hill, the Enfield Town Loop was temporarily reinstated.) The only parts to have been filled in are a short stretch behind Silver Street and the section between the Town Park and Bush Hill.

In 2002 the loop was thoroughly de-silted and refurbished. The only outstanding work at the time of writing is the short section alongside Southbury Road, where there have been persistent problems trying to keep the bed watertight - clay puddling would appear to be a lost art. At Bush Hill the River goes into Edmonton where it crosses the valley of Salmons Brook on an embankment built in the 1780s to replace a lead-lined timber aqueduct.

The original source from the Hertfordshire springs proved to be inadequate and the supply had to be augmented with water taken from the Lee below Hertford. During the 19th century the supply was further augmented by a series of deep boreholes and pumping stations - one of these stands alongside the New River at Goat Lane, Forty Hill.

In recent years the New River has been linked to the London Ring Main at Turnford (completed in 1994). Alongside the inner section between Turnford and Stoke Newington a series of boreholes has been sunk to enable water from the New River to be used to recharge the aquifer beneath London. The water stored in this fashion can be pumped back to the surface when required in times of drought. The scheme was completed in 1995. At the southern end the section between Stoke Newington and New River Head at Clerkenwell was abandoned after the last war, except for a short ornamental stretch through Islington - the New River Walk. Long stretches of the New River banks have been opened up to walkers in recent years and it still plays a significant role in London's water supply.

Sir John Robert Pretyman Newman

Newman (1871-1947) was Conservative MP for Enfield 1910-18. He won the seat from the Liberals in the election of 1910. Born in County Cork, he was of Anglo-Irish stock. During the First World War, despite being over military age, Newman served as a major in the Middlesex Regiment. In 1918, with his constituency boundaries altered, (Enfield had lost Edmonton, Southgate and Friern Barnet) Newman decided not to contest Enfield and instead stood successfully for Finchley, a seat he retained until 1924, when he was trounced by a Liberal.

North Lodge

A late 18th-century house built on Enfield Chase, North Lodge was for many years the home of the Gundry family. Just before the last war it was taken by the Kilvington Hall School. After the war it was acquired by Middlesex County Council for use as a remand home – St Nicholas House. Eventually, it was closed and sold; the building is now occupied by St John's School (a private school, not to be confused with St. John's Church of England School in Theobalds Park Road).

The North-South Road

This was planned to keep heavy industrial traffic away from Hertford Road. The scheme was devised well before the last war and the plans, as published in 1937, were substantially different from the road as built some fifty years later. It was intended to build the road along the Essex bank of the River Lee to link up with the proposed North Orbital Road (an early version of the M25) at Hoddesdon. Also considered was a northern extension to Great Chesterford to relieve the southern part of the A11 – an early version of what eventually materialised as the M11. Post war planners moved the road to the western bank of the Lee. Construction did not begin until 1985 and it was

115. The entrance hall of Old Park, now the club house of the Bush Hill Park Golf Club.

opened in stages after 1989. It incorporated Mollison Avenue, which had opened in 1964 at the same time as the link between Nag's Head Road and Lea Valley Road. A link to the M25 was omitted in order to keep down costs, thus seriously compromising the usefulness of the road. A recent unsuccessful attempt to revive this, the Northern Gateway Access Road, has met with sustained opposition because of the threat to the environmentally sensitive Ramney Marsh.

Old Park

A property of old, but uncertain date standing on top of Bush Hill. Once owned by the Clayton family, it was leased in 1809 to Rev. T. Winchester Lewis, whose widow, Elizabeth, bought the freehold in 1826. Old Park was later inherited by her son-in-law, **Edward Ford**, whose son, John Walker Ford, sold up in 1909. Old Park now survives as the club house of the Bush Hill Park Golf Club. Another portion of the Old Park Estate, severed by the Great Northern Railway's Enfield branch line of 1871, is now home to the Enfield Golf Club.

Old Park Road

At the time of enclosure (1803), this was a private road leading to Old Park Farm (now Enfield Golf Club). The Old Park Estate (Old Park Road, Crescent Road and Waverley Road) was developed for housing from 1880.

116. The eastern end of Ordnance Road under flood water in December 1914.

Ordnance Road

This was a road leading from Hertford Road to the Lee Navigation at Enfield Lock, and first known as Marsh Lane. Its previous names have included Welches Lane (from a former farmer), Lock Lane and Ordnance Factory Lane. The present name was in use by 1871, reflecting the close proximity of the Royal Small Arms Factory at Enfield Lock.

Palace Gardens Precinct

Various schemes to revitalise Enfield Town as a shopping centre have been put forward over a long period. In 1961 it was proposed to pedestrianise the Town and Church Street with traffic diverted on to an inner ring road, but concerns at the environmental effects of a ring road, which would massively damage St Andrew's churchyard and Holly Walk, led to the scheme being decisively rejected. Eventually plans were approved in 1979 for a shopping precinct south of Church Street on the Palace Gardens site. This opened in 1982 and helped to reverse the slow decline of Enfield Town as a shopping centre. A much delayed second phase, known as Palace Exchange, opened late in 2006, but it is currently too early to judge whether it will be successful.

Parks

Enfield Council's policy on parks and open spaces was remarkably far sighted. Before the First World War it acquired the Town Park (1901), Albany Park (1902), Durants Park (1903), North Enfield Recreation Ground (1907), Bush Hill Park Recreation Ground (1908), and Hilly Fields (1911). The programme resumed after the war with Ponders End Recreation Ground (1920), Whitewebbs (1931) and the King George Playing Field (1931). Since the last war the main acquisitions have been Forty Hall (1951) and Trent Park, which was transferred to the London Borough of Enfield in 1986 on the demise of its previous owner, the Greater London Council.

117. The bowling green at Durants Park.

118. An early shot of the Town Park viewed from the main gate in Cecil Road.

Parliamentary Representation

Prior to the Parliamentary Reform Act of 1832 Enfield was represented by the two county MPs for Middlesex. The polling place was The Butts, Brentford and voters had to turn up and vote in person. Within the county there were two borough constituencies: Westminster (with two MPs) and the City of London, which, because of its special status, elected four MPs.

After the Act, Middlesex, one of the most heavily populated constituencies in the country, was progressively sub-divided. In 1832 the Finsbury, Marylebone and Tower Hamlets Divisions were created, followed in 1867 by the Chelsea and Hackney Divisions. Finally in 1885 the rump of the old Middlesex County constituency was divided and one of the new constituencies formed was the Enfield Parliamentary Division. This covered a very large area: Enfield, Edmonton, Southgate, Friern Barnet and Potters Bar. As the population grew and the franchise was extended, further sub-division followed. In 1918 Edmonton became a separate seat and Southgate and Friern Barnet were joined with Wood Green (previously part of Tottenham) to form a new Wood Green constituency. Enfield was reduced to just Enfield and Potters Bar.

The 1948 Representation of the People Act set up the

Boundary Commission to continually review constituency boundaries. The first changes were implemented in time for the 1950 General Election. Southgate was split from Wood Green and Enfield was divided into Enfield East and Enfield West. Further changes followed in 1974 when Potters Bar was transferred to a new constituency of Hertfordshire South, later re-named Hertsmere. Large parts of Oakwood, Cockfosters, Hadley Wood and adjoining areas were moved from Enfield West into the Southgate constituency (renamed Enfield-Southgate). The remainder of Enfield West merged with Enfield East to form a new constituency confusingly called Enfield North. Since the General Election of 2005 more changes have been made. Ponders End has been moved from Enfield North to Edmonton and the whole of Highlands Ward (part of which was in Enfield-Southgate) is now included in Enfield North.

Parsonage Lane

So-called in 1754, the name derives from the former **Rectory (or Parsonage) Manor House**, which stood on the site now occupied by Monastery Gardens. The name was sometimes shortened to Parson's Lane.

119. A late 19th-century view of the north side of Parsonage Lane, looking east towards Baker Street.

Walter Pater

The art historian and novelist, Walter Pater (1839-94), was born in Poplar, where his father practised as a doctor. After his father's death, the family moved to Enfield, settling in a house at Chase Hill immediately to the west of Chase Green - they are listed at Chase Hill on the 1851 census. (The house was later demolished to make way for the Great Northern Railway's Cuffley extension.) Pater is believed to have briefly attended Enfield Grammar School, but the family later moved to Canterbury where he completed his education at the King's School before going on to Queen's College, Oxford. The rest of his life was spent almost entirely in Oxford. He is chiefly remembered today as the author of *Studies in the history of the English Renaissance* and a decidedly strange novel, *Marius the Epicurean*.

Frances Perry

Frances Perry (1907-93) was born Frances Mary Everett, at Bulls Cross. She was educated at Enfield County School and was introduced to horticulture by **Gussie Bowles**. She married a local nurseryman, Gerald Perry, the proprietor of Perry's Hardy Plant Farm and became a prolific writer of books on gardening. For many years she was the gardening correspondent of *The Observer*, a job that she inherited from Vita Sackville-West. She served on the Council of the Royal Horticultural Society from 1968, and the RHS awarded her the Veitch Memorial Medal in 1964 and the Victoria Medal of Honour in 1971. After the death of her first husband, she married Roy Hay, also a distinguished author of gardening books. Her brother, Denton Everett, was for many years licensee of the Pied Bull at Bulls Cross. On her death a substantial collection of books on gardening was bequeathed to the Capel Manor Horticultural College.

Phipps Hatch Lane

Named after a former gate to Enfield Chase, the Lane *(ill. 120)* formerly extended to Lavender Hill, including Cedar Road (briefly known as Cemetery Road) and part of Lavender Gardens.

William Pitt, Earl of Chatham

The Whig politician, William Pitt (1708-78), served as Paymaster General (1746-54). In 1756 he became Secretary of State, later combining that post with Leader of the Commons, in a government nominally led by the Duke of Newcastle. Pitt was responsible for Britain's strategy in the Seven Years War against France. The result was the end of French influence in India and the seizure of France's most valuable colony, Canada. Pitt was forced into resignation in 1761 because of disagreements over the direction of the war. By now Earl of Chatham, Pitt returned to power as Prime Minster 1766-68, but was then suffering from both gout and bouts of manic depression, and was unable to prevent the rapid deterioration of relations with the American colonies that was to lead to the American War of Independence. Later, appalled at the conduct of the war, he mercilessly harried Lord North's hapless government with memorable

120. *Phipps Hatch Lane c.1890. Many of the trees still survive along the edge of Hilly Fields.*

speeches in the House of Lords.

In 1747 he took a lease of South Lodge on Enfield Chase and remained there until 1753. During this time he carried out extensive work on the house and grounds. But the building suffered badly from damp and Pitt is reputed to have left after discovering a frog in his library. The house was demolished in 1935, but two lakes survive at Lonsdale Drive and Lakeside.

121. *Max Plowman. His former home in Rowantree Road is now the Enfield Hotel.*

122. *William Pitt the Elder (later Earl of Chatham).*

Max Plowman

Poet, literary critic and pacifist campaigner, Max Plowman (1883-1941) came from a family that originated in Finchley, but moved to Tottenham, where they established a successful brick making business. He was born in a house at Northumberland Park, Tottenham, but by the mid 1880s his family had moved to the prosperous Bycullah Estate at Enfield. The Plowmans lived initially in Culloden Road, but later moved to Lochnagar, a substantial house in Rowantree Road (now the Enfield Hotel). The Plowmans were staunch Congregationalists and had a long connection with Christ Church in Chase Side. Max's cousin, Tom Plowman, who also lived in Rowantree Road, was a leading figure in the Boys' Brigade movement in Enfield.

During the First World War Plowman served as a junior officer in the West Yorkshire Regiment, later being invalided out with shellshock. He later wrote *A Subaltern on the Somme* (1928), a simple and unadorned account of life in the trenches, probably re-worked from diaries. He also wrote some good quality war poems, one of the best of which, *The Dead Soldiers*, appears in many First World War anthologies.

After the war, he established himself as a respected literary critic and became editor of *The Adelphi*. He produced a major book on the poetry of William Blake that is still widely read today. His experiences of war led him inevitably towards pacifism. He and Canon Dick Sheppard helped to found the Peace Pledge Union and he later served as secretary of the organisation.

Plowman died in 1941 at his home in Essex, a disillusioned man, with his hopes of peace dashed. Sadly, there is no memorial to him in Enfield, but his cousin Tom is still remembered with affection at Christ Church United Reformed Church in Chase Side, where the Boys' Brigade unit is known as the Tom Plowman Troop.

Police

The Metropolitan Police area was extended outwards in 1840 to include Enfield and the old parish constables were finally displaced. A police station opened at Enfield Town in the Vestry House, which had been built in the 1830s as a combined watch house and beadle's house. (The building still stands and is now the office of the Old Enfield Charitable Trust.) Part of the premises served as living accommodation for the station sergeant and his family, but it soon proved inadequate and in 1867 a site was obtained for a new police station at the junction of Cecil Road and London Road. The new building, which included stables for mounted police, was

123. The former Enfield Town Police station of 1873 lying derelict in 1974.

largely complete by the end of 1872 and opened the following year. By 1939 this station, too, was officially regarded as inadequate and another site was acquired in Silver Street. However, because of the outbreak of war and subsequent financial stringency, progress in erecting a new building was painfully slow. Part of the site was used for a block of police flats called Oak House, but construction work on the new station did not begin until 1963 and the building opened in 1965. The old station in London Road was used briefly as a base for traffic wardens, but then lay derelict for some years prior to demolition in 1984.

There had been a police presence at Enfield Highway since at least 1849, operating from a building at Green Street. In 1866 land was purchased in Hertford Road opposite St James' Church and in 1868 the Enfield Highway Police station opened. In 1962 a site was acquired in Ponders End High Street, and in 1969 all facilities and services were transferred there. (An open day to show off the new building to local dignitaries was belatedly staged in 1970.) The old building at Enfield Highway has been sold off and is currently used for retail purposes.

Ponders End

Ponders End was a large hamlet in the parish of Enfield. The enclosure map of 1803 shows a straggling L-shaped settlement. The High Street was built up from Red Lane (Lincoln Road) to just south of Farm Lane (Southbury Road). Houses were dotted along South Street as far as Ponders End Mill and the Lee Navigation and there was a small settlement clustered around Scotland Green. There was then no road access across the river to Chingford. It was not until 1873 that Lea Valley Road was built, financed by public subscription.

In 1826 there were coaches every half hour to London, but in 1840 the first section of what was to become the main railway line to Cambridge was opened between Stratford and Broxbourne with a station at Ponders End. In 1845 this was served by 6 trains daily in each direction. In 1891 the opening of the Southbury Loop gave Ponders End a second station, sited in Southbury Road, but this line lost its passenger service in 1909 due to tramway competition.

In 1881 a horse tramway from Stamford Hill was opened as far as the junction of Southbury Road and the High Street. It did not prosper and within a short time the service was cut back to Tramway Avenue Depot at Edmonton. In 1907 a completely new electric tramway was built through Ponders End, reaching Waltham Cross in 1908 and in 1911 it was extended along Southbury Road, forming a branch to Enfield Town. Apart from the Southbury Road route the trams gave way to trolleybuses in 1938.

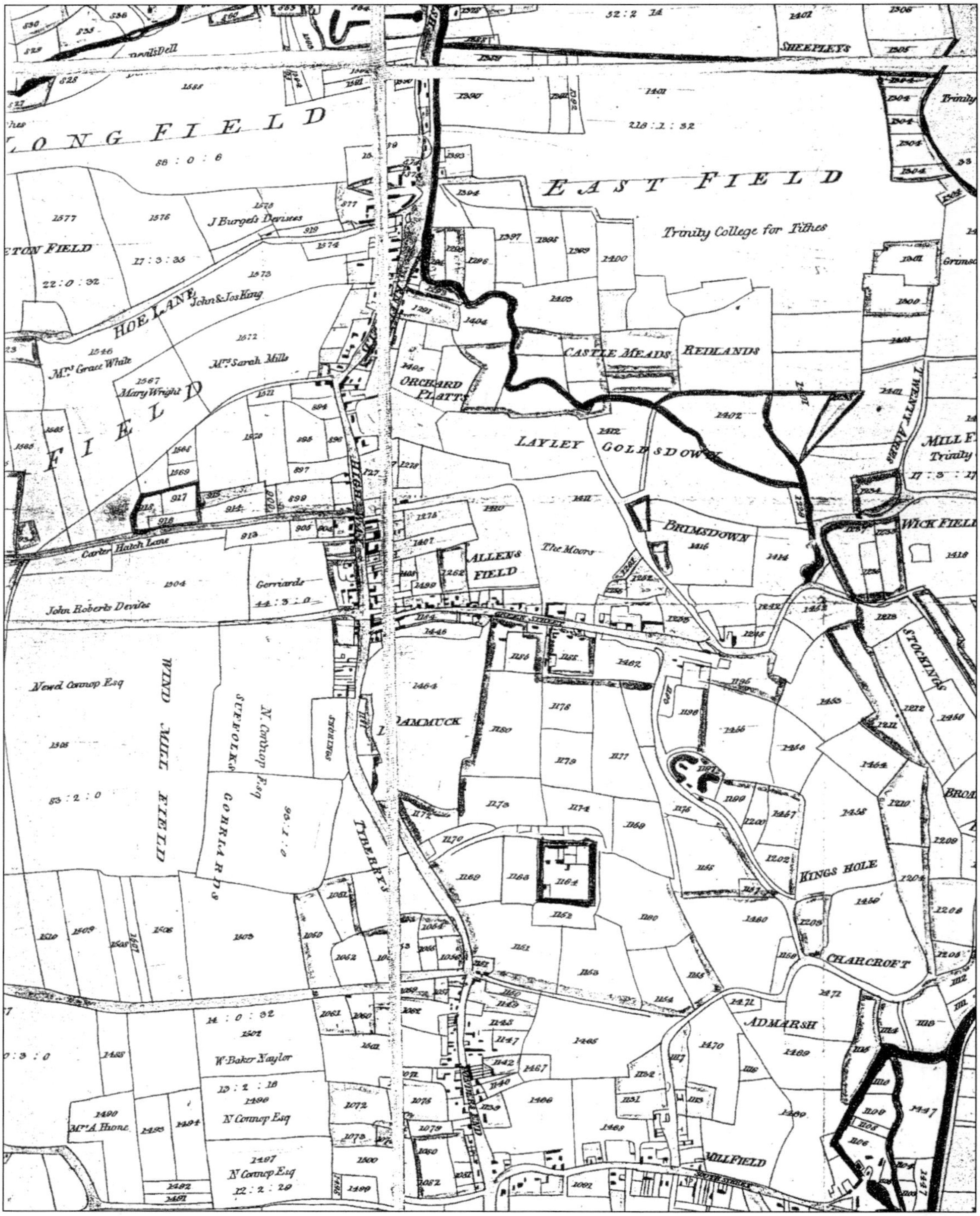

124. Ponders End and Enfield Highway in 1803.

125. An early 20th-century view of the centre of Ponders End at the junction of High Street and South Street. The Two Brewers (right) was bombed in 1940.

A report by the General Board of Health in 1850 on sanitary conditions in Enfield revealed an alarming state of affairs in Ponders End. Many of the older cottages were grossly overcrowded and extremely insanitary, the worst being in South Street and Scotland Green. The whole area suffered from poor drainage.

Housing development began at a fairly early date. Alma Road was developed from 1855 and Napier Road was laid out by 1867. The Lincoln House Estate (Derby Road and Lincoln Road) was built up from 1871 and Durants Road developed from 1888 and Nag's Head Road from 1890. By 1914 much of the area had been built up, but there was still open country separating Ponders End from Enfield Highway to the north, Edmonton to the south and Enfield Town to the west.

For many years the nearest church was at Enfield Town. Then in 1831 St James' church was built at Enfield Highway. Ponders End did not get a church of its own until 1878 when St Matthew's Church was erected in South Street. The nonconformists, however, took Ponders End rather more seriously – an Independent Chapel was built in the High Street in 1768, the direct ancestor of the present United Reformed Church in College Court.

The oldest industrial site is Ponders End Mill – the present buildings date from the late 18th century. In 1809 Grout and Baylis' crape factory was built in South Street. This closed in 1894 and the factory was later taken by United Flexible Metal Tubing. A jute mill was opened beside the Lee Navigation in 1865, lasting until 1882. Four years later it was occupied by Ediswan and used for the manufacture of electric light bulbs and radio valves. During the First World War a huge munitions factory, the Ponders End Shell Works, was built in Wharf Road; this was sold off after the war as a ready-made industrial estate. More factories were built in the thirties alongside the newly-built Great Cambridge Road.

Housing development resumed between the wars and the gaps between Ponders End and Edmonton and Enfield Highway were closed. By 1939 the area was virtually fully developed.

There have been several transport innovations since the last war. The Southbury Loop, closed to passengers since 1909, was re-opened and electrified in 1960. The Lea Valley Line was electrified in 1969. Trolleybuses gave way to conventional diesel buses in 1961. And in 1964 Nag's Head Road was extended to link up with Lea Valley Road, bypassing South Street and the heavily congested level crossing at Ponders End station.

From the 1950s there was much council redevelopment particularly in the South Street and Alma Road areas. Today Ponders End is an uneasy mixture of old and new: the Mill buildings survive in the shadow of the Alma Road tower blocks.

126. St Michael's Hospital, incorporating the former Enfield Workhouse of 1827.

Poor Law

During the second half of the 16th century there was a substantial rise in the numbers of poor and vagrants. These were people who, before the Reformation, had been dependent upon assistance from the Church and, in particular, the monasteries. This resulted in the passing of the 1601 Poor Law which, with later amendments, was to form the basis of poor relief in England until 1834. Each parish was made responsible for the support of those without the means to look after themselves. Parishes were required to appoint overseers of the poor, whose work was supervised by local magistrates, and were given powers to collect a rate from all occupiers of property to cover the costs.

Enfield established a workhouse in 1719 in rented premises to the east of Chase Side. The building was subsequently purchased in 1740 and was completely rebuilt and enlarged in 1827.

The 1834 Poor Law Amendment resulted in a reorganisation of poor relief with the twin aims of greater efficiency and reduced costs. Parishes were combined into Poor Law unions run by directly elected boards of guardians. Enfield became part of the Edmonton Poor Union, together with Tottenham, Hornsey, Edmonton, Cheshunt and Waltham Abbey. The Edmonton Board of Guardians took over from the parishes in 1837.

An Edmonton Union Workhouse was erected in Silver Street in 1842, enabling the former parish workhouses to be closed. However, the Enfield Workhouse, still a relatively new building, was too good to waste and was used to house the pauper children from the constituent parishes. This continued until 1886 when a purpose-built orphanage (the Chase Farm School) opened. The Enfield Workhouse was then used to house the aged and infirm.

The Poor Law was officially abolished by the 1929 Local Government Act and the functions of the Edmonton Board of Guardians were transferred to the Middlesex County Council.

However, much remains from the Poor Law. Parts of the Edmonton Union Workhouse (principally the 1910 infirmary block) survive, incorporated in the North Middlesex Hospital. Chase Farm Hospital includes substantial remnants of the 1886 Chase Farm School building and, more significantly, Poor Law attitudes are still deeply entrenched in the British Social Security system.

Prehistoric Enfield

The Enfield area was not hugely favourable to the activities of early man. The low-lying areas close to the River Lee were marshy and prone to flooding and the higher ground was thickly forested with oaks and hornbeams with a thick scrub of bramble and hawthorn at ground level. The trees would have been difficult to clear with the primitive tools available and the underlying soil was a stiff and soggy clay, highly resistant to early attempts at agriculture.

Archaeological evidence of the earliest period consists mainly of flint implements recovered from gravel deposits, often found in close proximity to the skeletal remains of prehistoric animals. This suggests a small population of hunter-gatherers living close to the river banks.

There is more evidence of the later Neolithic period. Polished stone axe heads have been found in gardens at Raith Avenue, Southgate and Connaught Avenue, Enfield, suggesting that the population was starting to move away from the river banks. From the Bronze Age, bronze artefacts, including spearheads, a sword and knife, have been found in gravel deposits at Edmonton Marsh and Ramney Marsh.

In the Iron Age the area came under the control of the Catuvellauni, a powerful tribe of Belgic origin, closely related in language and culture to the Gauls of France. Their kingdom was centred in Hertfordshire with settlements at Wheathampstead and St Albans, but later expanded eastwards when they conquered and absorbed their neighbours, the Trinovantes of Essex. From this period there survives the remains of two earthworks, one at Old Park (now the Bush Hill Park Golf Club) and the other at Hadley Wood much mutilated by the construction of the Great Northern Railway.

Railways

Enfield's railways developed over a period of nearly a hundred years, the oldest section opening in 1840 and the last addition being completed in 1933. They were built by two pre-1923 main line railway companies, the Great Eastern and the Great Northern, and the Underground Electric Railway Co. (later merged into London Transport).

127. Brimsdown Station, opened in 1844.

Great Eastern Railway

This was formed in 1862 by a merger of the Eastern Counties Railway with other companies serving East Anglia. The first section of the Eastern Counties was opened between Mile End and Romford in 1839 and from a junction with it at Stratford the Northern & Eastern Railway built the first part of their Cambridge main line, which opened as far as Broxbourne in 1840. This was constructed along the floor of the Lee Valley to reduce engineering costs, but with the unintended result that the stations were all well away from the main population centres – Enfield's first station was at Ponders End, and additional stations were at Ordnance Factory (Enfield Lock) (1855) and Brimsdown (1884).

In 1849 a single-track branch from the Cambridge line was opened from Water Lane (Angel Road) to Enfield Town with an intermediate stop at Edmonton Green (the old low-level station and not the current station). Its terminus was in Nag's Head Lane (Southbury Road) on the site of the present Enfield Town Station. (The original station house was adapted from a 17th-century house on the site previously used as a private school – John Keats had been a pupil there.) The line was constructed cheaply with the bare minimum of engineering works. A bridge was built at Edmonton Green (New Road) to avoid disruption to traffic on the Turnpike Road, but elsewhere level crossings were provided at Jeremy's Green Lane (Montagu Road), Edmonton Green, Bury Street and Red Lane (Lincoln Road). (The last mentioned survives and is a major source of aggravation to Enfield motorists.) The line was served mainly by a shuttle to and from Water Lane, but there were through trains to and from Bishopsgate in peak periods. Despite a roundabout route and the inconveniently located Bishopsgate terminus, the line stimulated some modest suburban development in both Enfield Town and Lower Edmonton. It also killed off the only competition, Glover's omnibus service, which ceased operation by 1855.

Soon after its formation the Great Eastern embarked upon a vigorous expansion of its sub-

128. *Ponders End Station c.1914. The buildings on the left dated back to the opening of the line in 1840.*

129. *The original Great Northern station on Windmill Hill opened in 1871. The site is now occupied by Gladbeck Way.*

urban services. In 1872 a new line opened from Bethnal Green to Lower Edmonton where it linked up with the original 1849 branch line, which was upgraded to double track between here and Enfield Town, where the terminus was rebuilt in rather grander style. In 1880 a new station was added at Bush Hill Park, where a new suburb was being built. In 1874 a new City terminus was opened at Liverpool Street, the former one at Bishopsgate becoming a freight depot.

The Company was required to run early morning workmen's trains at the unusually cheap fare of 2d. return. The result was a huge surge of working class population up both sides of the Lee Valley. In Enfield the effect was more muted, but significant numbers of working class houses were built in the Lancaster Road and Chase Side areas north of Enfield Town and the Lincoln Road and St Mark's Road area of Bush Hill Park.

Traffic on the new line grew fast and by the end of century was close to saturation point, the overcrowding particularly severe on the early morning workmen's trains. In Edmonton tempers boiled over early in 1899 with violent confrontations between workmen and ticket inspectors and railway police leading to the establishment of the Edmonton Workmen's Train Association. The result of the agitation was the somewhat grudging provision of some 3d. workmen's trains departing between 6.30 and 7 am.

Buoyed by the success of the new line, the company sought to expand further in the Enfield area. In 1891 the Edmonton and Cheshunt Line (now known as the Southbury Loop) opened between Bury Street Junction (south of Bush Hill Park) and Cheshunt on the Lea Valley Line. The line was built through mostly open country, ripe for development. There were three intermediate stations all constructed on substantial lines: Churchbury (Southbury), Forty Hill (Turkey Street) and Theobalds Grove. Traffic was light at first and the line was served by a shuttle between Cheshunt and White Hart Lane supplemented in peak hours by a few through trains to and from Liverpool Street. However, a new electric tramway to Waltham Cross (completed in 1908) led to a catastrophic haemorrhage of passenger traffic and a year later in 1909 the railway company gave up and withdrew the service. But in 1915 with the tramway along the Hertford Road struggling to cope with huge numbers of munitions workers, the passenger service was reinstated with the addition of a temporary halt at Carterhatch Lane. The line closed again in 1919, but was retained for freight traffic and as a diversionary route when the Lea Valley Line was closed by engineering work.

Traffic remained heavy and overcrowded on the Enfield Town and Chingford lines. In 1920 the Great Eastern responded with a complete reorganisation of its suburban services under the direction of its American-born General Manager, Henry Thornton, who had previously been General Superintendent of the Long Island Railroad. (Thornton must rank among the most dynamic and innovative railway managers ever to have worked in Britain.) The ideal solution would have been electrification, but financial constraints forbade this, and thus, any improvements were entirely dependent upon the more effective utilisation of existing locomotives and rolling stock. There were alterations to the signalling and track layout at the busy junctions at Hackney Downs and Bethnal Green and, to enhance capacity at Enfield Town Station, a third platform was added. At Liverpool Street the construction of a series of engine docks close to the platform ends dramatically reduced the turn round time for trains. The result was a ten-minute interval service on both the Enfield and Chingford line.

In 1923 the Great Eastern Railway was merged into the London & North Eastern Railway. Sadly, Henry Thornton was not retained by the new company and he returned across the Atlantic to become President of the Canadian National Railway. Apart from the provision of new locomotives and rolling stock, there were few changes to the pattern of services on the Enfield and Chingford line, but the ravages of the General Strike and the Second World War took their toll.

Great Northern Railway

The first section of the Great Northern's main line was opened in 1850 between London and Peterborough. It traversed the western edge of Enfield at Hadley Wood, but the company did not open a station here until 1885, and it is clear that not much local traffic was expected. The nearest GNR stations to Enfield were Colney Hatch (New Southgate), Barnet (New Barnet) and Potters Bar. In 1859 a station was opened at Wood Green, where a new suburb was growing up in what had hitherto been a fairly

130. Enfield Town Station in 1911. A third platform was added in 1920.

insignificant hamlet in the parish of Tottenham. In 1863 a connection was opened from King's Cross to the newly opened Metropolitan Railway enabling trains to be run initially to Farringdon (soon extended to Moorgate). From 1875 the North London Railway ran trains from Broad Street on the Great Northern via Canonbury and Finsbury Park.

In 1871 a branch was opened from Wood Green to Enfield with stations at Palmers Green and Winchmore Hill. This involved deep and substantial embankments to carry the line across the valleys of Pymmes Brook and Salmons Brook. The terminus at Enfield stood on the south side of Windmill Hill to the west of the present Enfield Chase Station on a site now covered by Gladbeck Way. It consisted of a long island platform covered by a wooden awning supported on cast iron columns, and fronting the road, a two-storey building incorporating a booking office and station master's house.

In order to relieve congestion on the main line caused by the tunnels at Hadley Wood and the Welwyn Viaduct, the company proposed to extend the Enfield branch northwards through Cuffley and Hertford, rejoining the main line south of Stevenage. Construction began in earnest in 1906 and involved an embankment across Chase Green, a deep cutting at Lavender Hill and a substantial viaduct across the valley of Turkey Brook south of Crews Hill. It was impossible to extend from the existing terminus, as this would have involved a level crossing on Windmill Hill and extensive property demolition on the affluent Bycullah Estate. Instead a new station (now Enfield Chase) was built slightly to the east on an embankment with sufficient height to cross Windmill Hill on a bridge. The extension was opened as far as Cuffley in 1910. As well as the new station on Windmill Hill, stations were provided at Gordon Hill and Crews Hill and on the original line a new one opened at Grange Park to serve the Old Park Grange Estate.

In 1904 the Great Northern announced plans for the electrification of its suburban lines. In connection with this it proposed to widen the line to four tracks between Bowes Park and Gordon Hill which would have been the terminus of the new electric trains. Gordon Hill Station was built with four platforms in anticipation of this role. In the event, the outbreak of the First World War killed off both schemes.

Construction north of Cuffley was slowed by shortages of manpower and materials during the war, but afterwards work resumed and the track was doubled, signalling installed, and the station buildings completed. The new line, now known as the Hertford Loop, was opened throughout for passenger traffic in 1924.

The Great Northern, like the Great Eastern, lost its identity in 1923, when it was merged into the London & North Eastern Railway. However, services continued in much the same pattern, with the inevitable disruptions caused by the Second World War, until well after nationalisation in 1948. The Piccadilly Line extension to Cockfosters took away much of the passenger traffic from the stations south of Palmers Green.

Nationalisation

The railways, near bankrupt and ravaged by war, were nationalised in 1948 and in 1955 plans were announced for the electrification of the lines from Liverpool Street to Enfield Town, Chingford, Hertford East and Bishops Stortford. (The line from Liverpool Street to Shenfield had been electrified in 1949 under a scheme initiated by the LNER before nationalisation and largely financed by the government.) To keep down costs the Lea Valley Line between Coppermill Junction and Cheshunt was omitted from the scheme, but it included the Southbury Loop, which had been more or less dormant since 1919. An electric service was introduced in the autumn of 1960 and at the same time the service on the Lea Valley Line went over to diesel traction. The locomotive depot alongside Enfield Town Station, whose smoke and ash had long been the subject of complaint, was closed and demolished

There were also proposals for the electrification of the suburban services emanating from King's Cross on the old Great Northern lines, but these were delayed by political indecision and financial problems. As a temporary measure diesel traction was introduced in 1959, and also that year the main line

131. The Piccadilly Line extension under construction in 1932. The bridge in the foreground carries the entrance to Oakwood Park from Lakenheath.

was widened through Potters Bar and Hadley Wood.

Electrification materialised in 1976 on the Hertford North and Welwyn Garden City services. At the same time the inner suburban services were mostly diverted to Moorgate (via the former Northern City tube line) and the services to Broad Street abandoned. The second phase was implemented in 1978 with electrification to Hitchin and Royston, subsequently extended to Peterborough, Cambridge and Kings Lynn.

The Piccadilly Line

The Piccadilly Line had its origins in three separate electric tube railways promoted in the late 19th century, which were merged as the Great Northern Piccadilly and Brompton Railway. By that time it had been taken under the wing of the Underground Electric Railway Co. presided over by the Chicago tramway millionaire, Charles Tyson Yerkes. Its most northerly station was at Finsbury Park.

Construction began in 1902 and it opened in December 1906. Soon after the First World War agitation began for a northern extension to relieve overcrowding on the existing suburban railways and to bring order to the chaotic interchange facilities with trams and buses at Finsbury Park. A northern extension from Finsbury Park to Cockfosters with stations at Manor House, Turnpike Lane, Wood Green, Bounds Green, Arnos Grove, Southgate, Enfield West and Cockfosters was sanctioned and this opened in stages from 1932 until July 1933, when Cockfosters was reached. The line is in a tunnel to just south of Arnos Grove, the rest being in the open, apart from a short tunnel at Southgate. It stimulated much housing development in the western part of Enfield.

In 1933 the line was taken over by the London Passenger Transport Board, the direct ancestor of Transport for London.

The stations on the Piccadilly extension, mostly designed by Dr Charles Holden, have proved to be a benchmark of modern architecture and many are now listed buildings. At Cockfosters the insignificant buildings at street level contrast sharply with the majestic concrete canopy covering the platforms.

Sir Nicholas Rainton

Rainton (1569-1646) came of Lincolnshire stock. He settled in London, first in Lombard Street and later in Cornhill, where he traded in silks, taffetas and velvets. He was prominent in the affairs of the Haberdashers' Company and in 1621 became a City of London Alderman for Aldgate Ward. He was elected Lord

132. Sir Nicholas Rainton, Lord Mayor of London 1632-3 and the first owner of Forty Hall.

133. John James Ridge, Enfield's first Medical Officer of Health.

Mayor in 1632, was later knighted, and was President of St Bartholomew's Hospital from 1634.

Rainton had a house in Enfield by 1620, possibly the Dower House at Forty Hill, but in 1629 on an adjoining site he commenced building a house in keeping with his greater status, **Forty Hall**, completed by about 1632 and which still retains many fixtures and fittings from his time.

Rainton, as a Puritan, found himself increasingly at odds with King Charles I in the period leading up to the outbreak of the Civil War. In 1640 the king, seriously embarrassed as a result of his military misadventures in Scotland, tried to extract money from the City of London by means of a forced loan. Rainton found himself briefly imprisoned for both refusing to lend money himself and to divulge details of the financial affairs of other City men. In 1642 after the outbreak of the Civil War, Rainton declined an offer of a place on the City's Committee of Safety and gradually eased his way out of City politics. He died in 1646 at Forty Hall and was buried in St Andrew's Church where his memorial (recently restored) can still be seen.

Rectory Manor House

This substantial house, of old but uncertain date, once owned by Trinity College, Cambridge, stood on the north side of Parsonage Lane. It was sold for building in 1926 and the site is now occupied by the misleadingly named Monastery Gardens. Some fine wrought iron gates were rescued and taken to Trinity College.

John James Ridge

John Ridge (1847-1908) was Medical Officer of Health for Enfield from 1881 until his death. He was born at Gravesend to a family of Sussex origin, who had been involved in medicine for several generations. He came to Enfield in 1872 when he took over the practice of Dr Benjamin Godfrey at Carlton House, Baker Street. He was a longstanding member of Christ Church Congregational church, a deacon, Sunday School superintendent and an active supporter of the Boys' Brigade. In politics he was a Liberal and was a friend of **George Spicer**, the Liberal chairman of the Enfield School Board and a fellow member of Christ Church. As Medical Officer of Health, Ridge was a brisk and hard working man and the scourge of local slum landlords. His most lasting achievement was in the field of hospital provision: the Enfield

134. *The Rectory Manor House, demolished to make way for Monastery Gardens.*

135. The Ridgeway looking north towards Chase Farm. In recent years the area has been over-developed with blocks of flats.

Isolation Hospital (later known as South Lodge) of 1900 and the earlier Enfield Cottage Hospital of 1875. His practice has survived to this day – after the demolition of Carlton House, it moved to new premises in nearby Tenniswood Road, where the current Head of Practice is his great grandson, Dr Tim Ridge.

The Ridgeway

This old track across The Chase was rebuilt as a fully fledged road after enclosure. It was sometimes known as Potters Bar Road. Always a major road, its importance has increased since the completion in 1984 of the M25 with which it connects at Potters Bar.

Rivers and Streams

The River Lee

The Lee is one of the many tributaries of the Thames and rises in Bedfordshire close to Luton. It forms the eastern boundary of Enfield and prior to 1965 marked the county boundary between Middlesex and Essex.

The river today is a mild-mannered affair with much of its flow diverted to supply London's drinking water. Its former propensity for flooding has been reduced by flood prevention measures carried out by the former Lee Conservancy Catchment Board. However, the size of the valley is indicative of a more dramatic past, being cut by the melt water from glaciers at the end of the last ice age. The same process left huge deposits of gravel and brick-earth which have been extensively worked in the Enfield area up to relatively recent times. *(See*

136. The River Lee near Enfield Lock with the inevitable group of small boys.

also separate entry for Lee Navigation)

The Boundary Ditch
A watercourse of uncertain origin which runs along the former Enfield/Edmonton boundary towards the Lee. Although it may originally have been natural in origin, the present course suggests that at the very least it has been straightened for much of its length. In more recent times its flow has been considerably augmented in times of wet weather by surplus water from the Saddlers Mill Stream diverted via a tunnel constructed by the former Lee Conservancy Catchment Board.

137. Salmons Brook downstream from Edmonton Green. The bridge carried the original railway line between Angel Road and Enfield Town (1849).

Pymmes Brook
This rises in Enfield at Hadley Wood, where it is joined near its source by a quaintly-named tributary, Monkey Mead Brook. It runs through East Barnet, Southgate, Palmers Green and Upper Edmonton before swinging southwards into Tottenham where it joins the Lee near Stonebridge Lock. The section alongside Angel Road was culverted as a flood prevention measure before the First World War. Further work (deepening, straightening and reinforcing the bank with concrete) was carried out in the Palmers Green area as a result of flooding in the disastrously wet summer of 1956.

Saddlers Mill Stream
This rises at the northern end of Chase Side, where it once took the drainage of the former workhouse. It passes beneath Parsonage Lane and across what is now the Enfield Grammar School playing field and under Holly Walk and Chapel Street. At this point it formerly fed a lake in the grounds of Little Park (now the Enfield Register office). The stream then passes beneath Church Street close to the Enfield Town Post Office, across the Town Park, under Uvedale Road, London Road, Village Road and Wellington Road. Passing under the railway line north of Bush Hill Park Station it then winds a circuitous course through the Bury Street and Bounces Road area before joining Salmons Brook. Saddlers Mill Stream is now entirely culverted except for a short stretch still open between London Road and Wellington Road. Flooding caused by this stream in the Bounces Road area led eventually to the construction of a diversionary tunnel taking surplus water to the Boundary Ditch at Ponders End. In 1859 pollution of the stream caused by a short-lived sewage works built by the Enfield Local Board of Health led to a fiercely contested court case in which the Edmonton Local Board of Health was granted an injunction preventing any further use of the watercourse as a sewage outfall.

Salmons Brook
This rises on Enfield Chase and soon after passing beneath Hadley Road, it is joined by two tributaries, Leeging Beech Gutter and Merryhills Brook, bearing the overflow from the lake at Trent Park. Below Slades Hill it crosses the Enfield Golf Course after being joined by another tributary bringing the overflow from Boxers Lake. At Grange Park it is joined by the Houndsden Gutter, which rises on the borders of Southgate and Cockfosters, and then passes under the railway embankment, The Chine, Old Park Ridings and the New River embankment at Bush Hill. (The course in this area was diverted and straightened before houses could be built in Park Drive.) Beyond this point the Brook goes under Ridge Avenue, Church Street, Little

138. The Turkey Brook running alongside Turkey Street. Early in 1881 a flood, caused by heavy rain and melting snow, resulted in sections of the road collapsing into the brook.

Bury Street, the Great Cambridge Road and across the Churchfield allotments. It then passes beneath Latymer Road, Winchester Road and the railway embankment north of Lower Edmonton Station to reach Edmonton Green. (Short sections have been culverted at Edmonton Green, between Winchester Road and the railway and either side of the bridge at Ridge Avenue.) Below Edmonton Green the present course (too straight to be natural) runs directly east to Montagu Road and then swings south to join Pymmes Brook near Angel Road.

Turkey Brook (Maidens Brook)
The brook rises just outside Enfield at Potters Bar, crosses Enfield Chase and passes beneath the railway at Rendlesham Viaduct. Passing through Hilly Fields, it is joined by a tributary, the Comreddy Gutter, which drains Lavender Hill Cemetery – the water has a distinctly organic smell at certain times of the year. Passing under Clay Hill it is joined on the eastern edge of Whitewebbs Golf Course by a substantial tributary, Cuffley Brook (as the name suggests this rises across the Hertfordshire border. Passing beneath Whitewebbs Lane, it feeds an ornamental lake in the grounds of Wildwoods. Close to Flash Lane it is spanned by a cast iron aqueduct that once carried an abandoned loop of the New River.) The combined streams cross the Forty Hall Estate feeding a chain of lakes, before passing under Maidens Bridge, the Great Cambridge Road and Turkey Street. It then runs alongside Turkey Street as far as the Woolpack Bridge beneath the Hertford Road. Between the Woolpack Bridge and the Lee the present course is an artificial cut made in the early 19th century. The original course ran south along the east of the Hertford Road before swinging eastwards towards Bell Lane – much of this survives underground as part of the surface water drainage system.

William Robinson

Enfield's first historian, the author of *The History and Antiquities of Enfield* (1823). Robinson (1777-1848) was born illegitimate, his mother reputedly being a sister of Lord Nelson. He became a lawyer, qualifying as an attorney in 1798, and in 1803 he married Mary Ridge, the daughter of a Chichester banker. In 1821, by now largely retired, he moved to Tottenham, at long last able to indulge his interest in local history. In addition to his work on Enfield, he published histories of Tottenham, Edmonton, Stoke Newington and Hackney. He also left in varying stages of completion unpublished histories of Hornsey, Hampstead and Stepney.

His book on Enfield is in two volumes, not particularly well organised and written in a somewhat pedantic style. His

139. Enfield Town's first Roman Catholic church (in London Road) was opened in 1901 and demolished after bomb damage in 1940.

work is of value where he is quoting from documents that either no longer exist or are now inaccessible to researchers.

140. The Church of Our Lady of Mount Carmel and St George, which replaced its bombed predecessor in 1958

Roman Catholicism

The revival of Roman Catholicism in Enfield dates from the mid-19th century and appears to be linked with the Irish Potato Famine of 1845-48, which caused large scale Irish migration to the British mainland. A small chapel was built in Cecil Road in 1863, moving to a much larger building in London Road in 1901. This was destroyed by a landmine in 1940 and was replaced by the present church in 1958. East Enfield was originally served from Waltham Cross, but a chapel was later built in Alma Road; St Mary's Church, Nag's Head Road dates from 1921. The western edge of Enfield is served by the Benedictine Church of Christ The King (1940), which stands just inside the former Southgate boundary at Bramley Road.

Roman Enfield

Julius Caesar led expeditions to Britain in 55BC and 54BC during the course of which his army may have penetrated as far north as Wheathampstead. Finally, in AD43 the Emperor Claudius launched an invasion of Britain and much of southern England was quickly overrun and settlements founded at Colchester (*Camulodunum*), London (*Londinium*) and St Albans (*Verulamium*). Enfield would have been among the first parts of the country to come under Roman rule.

In AD60 Boudicca, Queen of the Iceni, a tribe based in Norfolk, led a revolt against Roman rule. With the Roman forces heavily engaged in the conquest of North Wales and Anglesey, the insurgents met little serious opposition and within a short time overran much of southern England north of the Thames. Colchester, London and St Albans fell to the rebels in quick succession – the towns were burned and their inhabitants massacred. However, the Romans brought their forces back from Wales and Boudicca's army was decisively defeated. During the rebellion Enfield lay in territory under the control of the insurgents.

Ermine Street, the Roman road from London to York, traversed Enfield, but the only part of the alignment still in use today is a short stretch at Bulls Cross. A Roman settlement grew up alongside the road at Bush Hill Park. In 1902 Roman pottery and artefacts were discovered during the construction of Landseer Road and a lead coffin was found at Burleigh Road. Much more

Roman material came to light in excavations conducted in 1974-76 in conjunction with the redevelopment of The Avenues.

Further north there is evidence of a Roman settlement at Cheshunt. Another settlement has been excavated at Braughing, where Ermine Street intersected Stane Street, the Roman road from St Albans to Colchester.

The last Roman forces were withdrawn from Britain in AD410 as Rome itself came under threat, but some semblance of organised government clearly survived for some time after this date. In AD429 and AD448 Germanus, Bishop of Auxerre, was able to travel to Britain and visited London and St Albans. Both cities, though clearly in terminal decline, were still fit to receive a foreign visitor. The Saxon invasion of Kent began in earnest in AD449 and by 457, after the Battle of Crayford, the control of the area south of the Thames passed out of British control. However, progress northwards was much slower and it was only after the Battle of Bedford (571) that it can be certain that the area north of the Thames came firmly under Saxon jurisdiction. There is no evidence of continuity in Enfield, as the Bush Hill Park settlement appears to have been completely abandoned and a new settlement was founded at Enfield Town.

The Royal Small Arms Factory

The factory replaced an earlier plant at Lewisham and came into production in 1816, just too late to affect the outcome of the Napoleonic War. It was designed by **John By** with some assistance from Sir John Rennie. A shortage of weapons during the Crimean War (1854-5) resulted in the factory being reorganised on mass production lines modelled on the Springfield Armoury, Massachusetts.

The products included the Enfield Rifle (used in the Crimean War), the Martini-Henry Rifle (used in the Zulu War) and the Lee-Enfield rifle (Boer War). An adapted version of the latter, the Short Magazine Lee-Enfield, was to be a standard British infantry weapon in both world wars. Also made here was a carbine for the Indian Army, the ammunition for which, packed in tallow, made from refined animal fat, proved unacceptable to both Hindu and Moslem soldiers, and inadvertently helped to fuel the Indian Mutiny of 1857.

The highly skilled workforce was well paid and politically aware. It was these men who in 1872 set up the **Enfield Highway Co-op**. Apprentice training at the RSAF was of a very high standard and many former apprentices went on to hold key positions in British industry.

The end came in 1988 shortly after the government had sold the factory to British Aerospace. A few buildings have been preserved, but the rest were cleared to make way for a housing development misnamed Enfield Island Village.

141. Outside the main gates of the Royal Small Arms Factory before the First World War.

Saint Andrew's church

The dedication to St Andrew and the presence of a resident priest at the time of Domesday (1086) both indicate an early date and it is almost certain that there was a church on this site in Anglo-Saxon times. However, nothing as early as this survives in the present building. Much of the chancel dates from the 13th century. The nave arcades and the tower are of the 14th century and the north aisle of the 15th century. The clerestory above the nave arcades was added in the early 16th century - note the Tudor rose and the wing badge of Sir Thomas Lovell. The south aisle and porch were rebuilt in brick in 1826. The older parts were built mainly of Kentish ragstone, but with some flint in the tower.

The building is by Middlesex standards large - the church of a small market town rather than a village. Although it has been much restored and all the roofs renewed, it remains impressive. It contains a substantial collection of monuments, including those of **Sir Nicholas Rainton** (1646) and a brass to Joyce Tiptoft (mother of John Tiptoft, Earl of Worcester). The organ case dates from 1752. The rood screen has long vanished, but the stair turret that gave access to the loft above survives in the north aisle. The pews date from 1854, installed amid great controversy by the then vicar, **John Moore Heath**. The churchyard is large and, despite some fairly drastic tidying up, retains many interesting monuments including those to **George Hodson, John Moore Heath** and **David Waddington**.

142. St Andrew's church in the late 19th century, showing the pews that the Rev. Heath controversially installed.

Sir Philip Sassoon

On his father's side, Sassoon (1888-1939) was descended from a Sephardic Jewish family long resident in Bombay. His mother was of Ashkenazi Jewish stock from the French branch of the Rothschild family. In 1912 on the death of his father, he inherited **Trent Park**, which his father had purchased from the **Bevan** family in 1908. Also in 1912 he was elected as Conservative MP for Hythe and held the seat until his death. During the First World War he was private secretary to Field Marshal Sir Douglas Haig. Afterwards he resumed his political career, serving as Under Secretary for Air (1924-29 and 1931-37) and First Commissioner of Works (1937-39). A man of immense wealth and refined taste, Sassoon virtually rebuilt Trent Park, using 18th-century bricks and a staircase salvaged from Devonshire House in Piccadilly. The house was used for lavish entertainment of the rich and powerful.

On his death Sassoon was cremated and the ashes scattered from an aircraft over the Trent Park Estate. One of his cousins was the poet, Siegfried Sassoon (1886-1967). His sister, Sybil, married the Marquis of Cholmondley and went to live at Houghton Hall in Norfolk.

Schools

Before the 1870 Education Act most schooling was in church hands - the National Society (C. of E) and the British Society (nonconformist).

Church Schools

St James's School opened in Hertford Road in 1833 and Ponders End (now St Matthew's) and Trent both began in 1838. These were followed by St Andrew's (1839), Forty Hill (1851), Holly Bush (1865), Ordnance Road (1874) and St John's (1889).

The Enfield British School in Chase Side opened in 1838 and there was another short-lived British School at Enfield Highway. Catholics opened St Mary's School in Alma Road in

143. Chesterfield Road School was opened by the Enfield School Board in 1897. The building has lasted well.

1888 (later moving to Durants Road) and St George's in Cecil Road in 1903 (later moving to Gordon Road).

An Anglican comprehensive school, Bishop Stopford, opened in 1967 in the former Suffolks Secondary Modern building. St Ignatius, a Jesuit-run boys' grammar school founded at Stamford Hill in 1894, went comprehensive and moved to Enfield in 1968. There was no secondary school for Catholic girls until the Holy Family Convent, founded as a private school, was brought into the state system after 1944. (Now comprehensive, this has merged with St Angela's School, Palmers Green and been renamed St Anne's.)

School Board and Education Committee

The Enfield School Board (established in 1894) implemented a massive school building programme, continued after 1903 by the Education Committee: Bush Hill Park (1896), Chesterfield (1897), Alma (1897), Chase Side (1901), Southbury (1905), Eastfield (1909), Lavender (1910), George Spicer (1912) and Botany Bay

144. A class at St Andrew's School, Sydney Road, in 1911. The headmaster, Edward Dugdale (right), was the father-in-law of Thomas Hardy.

145. A class at Carterhatch School soon after opening in 1949.

(1914). A second building programme began in the 1930s but was cut short by the last war: Suffolks (1934), Brimsdown (1939) and Merryhills (1940).

Enfield Grammar School *(see separate article)* was lured into the state system, accepting its first grant in 1893. A girls' grammar school, Enfield County, opened on an adjoining site in 1909 and in 1920 the Enfield Central School was established, using part of the George Spicer building. Two senior elementary schools (prototype secondary moderns) opened at Suffolks (1934) and Albany (1939).

1944 onwards

The post-war period saw a huge demand for school places met by a large building programme. New primary schools were built at Carterhatch (1949), Prince of Wales (1950), Grange Park (1951), Honilands (1953), Worcesters (1954), Capel Manor (1958) and Hadley Wood (1965). New secondary schools included two secondary moderns: Chase Boys (1956) and Chase Girls (1962), and a technical grammar, Ambrose Fleming (1962). Enfield's secondary schools went comprehensive in 1967 amid great political controversy. New comprehensives built since include Kingsmead (1967), Bullsmoor (1977) and Highlands (2000) - the first school to be completed under the government's private finance initiative. Chase Boys is now coeducational and Ambrose Fleming was closed to free the building for use by Enfield College.

Scotland Green Road

This runs north-east from South Street towards Millmarsh Lane. The name Scotland Green was in use by 1754 - there is also a Scotland Green in Tottenham. There was formerly an area called Ireland Green on the opposite side of South Street.

Silver Street

This street *(ill. 146)* is the principal road leading north from Enfield Town. The 1754 Tithe Map and the 1803 Enclosure Map both show it as part of **Baker Street** – the two names appear to have been more or less interchangeable, but Silver Street appears to have got the upper hand by 1826. In 1572 both Silver Street and the southern part of Baker Street were known as Parsonage Street – not to be confused with Parsonage Lane.

Sir Osbert Sitwell

The poet and short story writer, Osbert Sitwell (1892-1969) was a member of a remarkable literary family – his sister was the poet Dame Edith Sitwell and his brother the poet and architectural historian Sacheverell Sitwell. Before Eton, he was educated at the Ludgrove School at Cockfosters where he was unhappy. Many years later he recalled this time in *The Scarlet Tree*, part of his multi-volume autobiography. In the 1930s, he returned to Cockfosters in rather happier circumstances as a guest of **Sir**

146. Silver Street looking north towards The Town.

147. Sir Alfred Somerset of Enfield Court.

Philip Sassoon at Trent Park. His final years were sad, ravaged by the symptoms of Parkinson's Disease, and spent mostly in Italy, where he died.

Sir Alfred Plantagenet Somerset

The grandson of the 5th Duke of Beaufort and nephew of Field Marshal Lord Raglan, British commander in the Crimean War, Somerset (1829-1915) settled in Enfield in 1852, when he inherited **Enfield Court** from his godfather, General John Martin, a Waterloo veteran. He was Master of the Enfield Chase Staghounds and a great coaching enthusiast, for some years running his own coach, *The Hirondelle*, between Enfield and Hitchin. He was the commander of the local volunteers, the direct ancestor of the Territorial Army. Somerset *(ill. 147)*, a pillar of respectable society, must have been more than slightly embarrassed by the activities of his cousin, Lord Arthur Somerset, who moved abroad in some haste after being implicated in the Cleveland Street Scandal of 1889-90.

Eileen Soper

Soper (1905-90) was born at Reddaford, a house (now demolished) in Slades Hill. Her father was George Soper, a watercolour artist and wood engraver specialising in pictures of horses. Eileen became an accomplished wildlife artist, but she will probably be best remembered for the illustrations and book covers that she did for Enid Blyton's books, including the Famous Five series. The family moved from Enfield, settling at Harmer Green, Hertfordshire. She was a cousin of the Scottish Olympic athlete

148. South Lodge, demolished in 1935.

Eric Liddell, so memorably portrayed in the film, *Chariots of Fire*.

South Lodge

One of the lodges on Enfield Chase, the house was leased to **William Pitt** (later Earl of Chatham) for six years from 1747. In its last years the house was a private school, one of the pupils at which was the writer, Edward Sackville-West. The house was demolished in 1935 when the estate was sold to Laing's for housing. (The site of the house lay at the junction of Merryhills Drive and Greystoke Gardens.) From the landscaping there survives the lakes at Lakeside and Lonsdale Drive and some unusual trees now still flourishing in back gardens.

South Street

One of the principal streets in Ponders End, leading east from the High Street to the mill and the River Lee. It became part of a through road to Chingford in 1873 with the opening of the Lea Valley Road. With the diversion of the latter to link up with Nag's Head Road in 1964, and the subsequent closure of the railway level crossing, South Street has become something of a backwater. The name was in use by 1572.

Southbury Road

This road *(ill. 150)* is the principal east-west road linking Enfield Town with Ponders End. Prior to enclosure in 1803 it existed as two small lanes, one from Ponders End and the other from Enfield Town, linked by a footpath. The eastern end was known as Farm Lane and the western variously as Nag's Head Lane (from a former pub) or Oldbury Lane (from a former moated site). After enclosure the footpath section was upgraded into a fully fledged road, known throughout as Nag's Head Lane. In 1882 the Enfield Local Board of Health re-named it Southbury Road (from an adjoining field). A minority on the Local Board wanted to call it Great Eastern Road.

149. South Street early in the 20th century. The view looks east towards the station.

150. Southbury Road c.1923 looking east. Note the junction with the as yet uncompleted Great Cambridge Road.

The board schools were built to the highest standards of the time and it is no surprise to learn that all remain in use and are in better condition than many more recent school buildings. After his death, the George Spicer School in Southbury Road (1912) was named after him.

Strayfield Road

This was a former access road to The Chase, known in 1572 as Moorhatch Gate Street. It is now a cul-de-sac petering out into a footpath across Crews Hill Golf Course.

George Spicer

Spicer (1854-1911) was born at Woodford, Essex, the son of James Spicer, a wealthy papermaker. (The firm of Spicer's was to last for many years, eventually becoming part of the Reed Group - the Spicer trade name is still used.) George Spicer later settled in Enfield in a large Victorian house, Dunraven, on The Ridgeway. He was a member of Christ Church Congregational church and an active Liberal. In 1894, with the formation of the Enfield School Board, Spicer successfully stood for election to the new body. He led the Progressives (i.e. Liberals) on the School Board and became chairman after the second School Board election of 1897. He remained chairman until the disbandment of the Board in 1903, subsequently becoming the first chairman of the Enfield Education Committee which took over in the same year, remaining in post until 1907. It is no exaggeration to say that Spicer set the tone of state education in Enfield.

151. George Spicer, chairman of Enfield School Board.

Swimming Pools

An indoor heated swimming pool was built by the Enfield Local Board of Health in 1893 at Bradley Road, Enfield. Previously local swimmers had used the River Lee and there were the inevitable accidents and the local press reported many inquests on drownings. The pool was replaced in 1990 by the Albany Pool, built on the edge of Albany Park fronting on to Hertford Road. In 1932 an open air pool was built in Southbury Road on a site originally intended for a council depot. It was well equipped

152. The former Southbury Road swimming pool at the height of its popularity.

153. The tram terminus in Enfield soon after opening in 1909.

and laid out on generous lines, but in later years it fell on hard times. As a facility that could be used only for half the year it inevitably attracted unfavourable attention from a cash-strapped local authority. It was initially closed 'temporarily', but there was clearly no intention of ever reopening it, and in 1998 the long derelict remains were demolished.

Robert Stammers Tabor

Tabor (1819-1909) was born at Colchester, educated at Trinity College, Cambridge and ordained into the Church of England. In 1844 he was appointed curate-in-charge of Christ Church, Cockfosters, which had been built and endowed by Robert Cooper Lee Bevan of Trent Park. In 1854, when his parish was hit by an outbreak of cholera, Tabor complained bitterly about the inadequate response of the Enfield Local Board of Health. In the field of education he took a great interest in the work of the Trent National School and he also took fee-paying pupils at the Vicarage. In 1856 he abandoned the Church for full-time educational work when he took over the running of Cheam School with financial assistance from Robert Cooper Lee Bevan, who was a partner in Barclays Bank. By the time Tabor retired as headmaster in 1890 he had transformed Cheam from an ailing establishment into one of the country's leading preparatory schools. He was succeeded by his son, Arthur Tabor, who was headmaster until 1920.

Theobalds Park Road

Built after the 1803 enclosure of The Chase, it links Clay Hill to Cattlegate Road and Whitewebbs Lane. On 19th-century census records it was frequently treated as an extension of Clay Hill.

Tramways

In 1881 the North London Suburban Tramways Co., established three years earlier, opened a horse tramway between Stamford Hill and Edmonton with a depot at Tramway Avenue. A year later an extension was built along Ponders End High Street as far as the junction with Southbury Road, but plans for a further extension to Waltham Cross were abandoned in 1883. But, as business

154. *The temporary tram terminus outside the Green Dragon, Winchmore Hill in 1907. The line was extended to Enfield Town in 1909.*

155. *The last tram outside The George at Enfield Town, 1938.*

was good at the southern end of the route, it was opened along Seven Sisters Road to Finsbury Park (1885) and from Manor House to Wood Green via Green Lanes (1887).

In 1887 the company abandoned horses in favour of steam trams: passenger carrying trailers hauled by miniature steam locomotives with the moving parts skirted to protect other road users. Although mechanically successful, the new vehicles were soon found to be too heavy for the track, resulting in broken rails. The ongoing problems brought about the bankruptcy of the tramway company in 1891, the routes being taken over by the North Metropolitan Tramways Co. The new owners immediately reverted to horses, but this was clearly not a long term answer. The section through Ponders End was abandoned at this time.

In 1901 the routes were taken over for rebuilding and electrification by another new company, Metropolitan Electric Tramways. The section from Finsbury Park to Tottenham via Seven Sisters Road was electrified in 1904 followed a year later by the route through Edmonton to Tramway Avenue. It was then extended rapidly northwards along Ponders End High Street and Hertford Road reaching Freezywater (Woolpack Bridge) in 1906 and Waltham Cross in 1908.

In 1904 the route from Manor House to Wood Green was also electrified and extended northwards along Green Lanes reaching the Green Dragon at Winchmore Hill in 1907. With the old main road over Bush Hill unsuitable for tramcars, the tramway went through Enfield Town via Village Road and Park Avenue (both upgraded residential roads) and a specially constructed link road (Ridge Avenue). The line opened in 1909, terminating in front of The George.

In 1911 a branch opened from Ponders End to Enfield Town via Southbury Road. This went to a temporary terminus a short distance to the east of Enfield Town station. The intention was to link up with the other line outside The George, but by the time the necessary road widening in Southbury Road had taken place, the abandonment of London's trams in favour of buses was already well advanced and the link was never made.

Metropolitan Electric Tramways was taken over in 1933 by the newly formed London Passenger Transport Board and within a short time plans were made to convert the tram-

156. Trolleybuses close to the Waltham Cross terminus, sharing the road with a wartime Home Guard parade.

ways to trolleybus routes, with electrically powered vehicles using power from overhead wires. Both the Enfield tram routes were switched to trolleybus operation in 1938, but the Southbury Road branch was not deemed worthy of conversion and was completely abandoned. The redundant trackwork was mostly removed for scrap during the last war.

Trolleybuses

In 1938 Enfield's tramways, other than those on the Southbury Road branch, were converted to trolleybus operation. The tramway overhead power supply was modified by the addition of a second wire to carry the return current which had previously been directed via the running rails.

The vehicles were fast, smooth-running and quiet, the last quality being appreciated by people living alongside tram routes, but this could be a danger to unwary pedestrians. Although more manoeuvrable than the trams they replaced, they were still tied to the overhead power supply and tended to 'bunch', causing traffic congestion. In the mid 1950s, with overhead wires becoming more difficult to maintain, the decision was made to abandon trolleybuses in favour of ordinary diesel buses. In Enfield the change-over was made in 1961. The redundant wiring was quickly removed, but some of the supporting poles, which also carried street lamps, lasted a little longer. With air pollution from traffic fumes now a major source of concern, it is possible that the wrong decision was made.

John Tuff

John Tuff (1801-71) was the author of *Historical, Topographical and Statistical Notices of Enfield* (1852). Born in Stilton in Huntingdonshire, he was by profession a pharmacist with

157. John Tuff, pharmacist and local historian.

158. John Tuff's pharmacy on the right, near The George, c.1870. Charles Lamb was a customer.

159. The Plough, Turkey Street in 1974. It was demolished in 2002 before English Heritage could get the building listed.

a shop in Enfield Town close to The George, established by 1826. His book is poorly written and arranged and with a truly appalling index, but, by recording many things that were common knowledge at the time, Tuff has done a great service to later historians.

Turkey Street

Previously known as Tuttle Street (1695) and Tuckey Street (1789). Once a through road from Bulls Cross to Enfield Wash, it is now severed by the central reservation of the A10.

United Reformed Church

The Church was formed in 1972 by a merger of the Congregational Church with the Presbyterian Church of England. In Enfield the Congregationalists were definitely the senior partner. There was just one Presbyterian Church in Enfield, St. Paul's in Old Park Avenue (1902), once well supported and with a large number of emigré Scots among its membership. By the time it joined the URC membership was in decline and it eventually merged with Enfield Methodist Church, now called Trinity Church. Ponders End Congregational Church was a chapel dating from 1768, bombed in 1940 and replaced by the present building at College Court in 1959. Christ Church, Chase Side started in 1780 as a chapel affiliated to the Countess of Huntingdon's Connexion, but later joined the Congregationalists - the present church dates from 1875. Other Congregational churches were built at Lancaster Road (1885), Main Avenue, Bush Hill Park (1910) and Freston Gardens, Cockfosters (1939).

David Waddington

Waddington (1810-63) was born in Ardwick, Manchester, the son of an iron founder. His first involvement in railway af-

160. Christ Church Congregational church (now United Reformed) in Chase Side. The building dates from 1875.

fairs came when he joined the board of the Manchester and Birmingham Railway, one of a group of companies under the control of George Hudson, the so-called Railway King. In 1845 Hudson became chairman of the ailing Eastern Counties Railway with Waddington as vice chairman and chairman of the traffic committee. Under new management the company apparently prospered and dividends rose, but the methods used were highly questionable. It subsequently emerged that, on Hudson's orders, dividends were being paid from the company's share capital and that Waddington had been doctoring the accounts to make it appear that the money had been earned. By 1848 the financial state of the company was such that no sleight of hand on the part of Hudson and Waddington could possibly conceal it. With a shareholders' meeting due, Hudson decamped, leaving Waddington to face the shareholders alone. Both men were ejected from the board. Hudson's career was shattered, but Waddington, displaying a remarkably thick skin, was later recalled to the board and elected chairman in 1851. He maintained a precarious hold on the chair until 1856 when he was again ejected amid suspicions of malpractice.

In 1847 Waddington was

161. Adelaide House, Forty Hill, home of David Waddington. It was demolished in 1938 and the pond has since been filled in.

162. Walter Warwick, founder of Hadley Wood Golf Club.

163. The boilers at the former Alma Road pumping station.

elected as Tory MP for Maldon, just as the Eastern Counties Railway was about to open a branch line to the town. The campaign was a dirty one with large numbers of voters being placed on the company pay roll in the weeks before the election. In 1852 he was elected in a similar fashion for the neighbouring Essex constituency of Harwich, which he represented until 1857.

By 1848 he had settled in Enfield at Adelaide House, Forty Hill, which was to be his home for the next nine years. He was a trustee of the Forty Hill National School and 1853 he became Vicar's Warden at St Andrew's Church just in time to get embroiled in the Pew Controversy of 1853-4. Waddington worked closely with the Vicar, **John Moore Heath** and thus found himself the target of much local abuse and vilification. (A contemporary verse refers to Waddington as 'the Manchester upstart'.) In April 1854 feelings ran so high at a Vestry meeting that a fist fight broke out between Waddington and another Vestry member, Daniel Harrison. Waddington left Enfield in 1857, moving first to Redhill, Surrey and later to Bromley, Kent, where he died. His body was brought back to Enfield, where he was buried with his wife and a son who had both predeceased him. His monument still survives in the northern extension of St Andrew's churchyard, but was heavily obscured by ivy when last viewed by the author.

Wagon Road

So called on the 1867 Ordnance Survey map, this road was sometimes known as Long Hill. It originated as a trackway across The Chase linking Cockfosters Road with Gannick Corner on the Great North Road. Opinions vary as to whether the name should be spelt Wagon or Waggon.) Prior to the enclosure of The Chase it continued to the east of Cockfosters Road linking up with East Lodge Lane.

Walter Curry Warwick

Warwick (1877-1963) was a leading figure in British shipping. He was born in West Hartlepool, came to London in 1896 and joined the staff of the Furness Withy Line, the beginning, as it turned out, of a spectacularly successful career in shipping. He served as a director of Houlder Brothers, the Shaw Savill Line, Royal Mail Line and Pacific Steam Navigation. Later he became Chairman of Houlder Brothers and Pacific Steam Navigation.

Warwick settled in Hadley Wood in 1919 at Walmar (later no. 56) Beech Hill. He and fellow shipping magnate, Frederick Lewis (later Lord Essendon) were the co-founders of the Hadley Wood Golf Club, set up on the Beech Hill Park Estate. The newly formed club opened for business in May 1922.

Water Supply

Although the **New River** passed through Enfield, apart from a few properties adjoining the river that exercised dipping rights, it made no contribution to Enfield's water supply, which was largely dependent upon shallow wells. By 1850, when the General Board of Health carried out an inspection of Enfield, most of these were polluted in varying degrees, causing public health problems.

When the Enfield Local Board of Health was established in 1850, one of its first priorities was water supply. In 1855 on a site at Alma Road, Ponders End a deep well was bored through to the chalk aquifer below the clay and gravel and a pumping station was built, and a reservoir was built at the top of Holtwhites Hill. By April 1856 the waterworks was sufficiently complete to be shown off to a visiting inspector from the General Board of Health, Alfred Dickens, brother of the novelist. Despite early optimism, the system in its early days was dogged by mechanical problems with the pumps and leaking mains. A second well and pumping station was later built behind Eagle House in Ponders End High Street and a second reservoir to serve the eastern half of Enfield was built on the north side of Southbury Road. In 1885 a water tower was built next to the Holtwhites Hill Reservoir to give increased pressure in the mains. In 1904 the whole installation was sold to the newly formed Metropolitan Water Board, passing to Thames Water in 1974. The only remaining relic of the former Enfield Waterworks is the Holtwhites Hill Reservoir.

In addition to the above, the following organisations have been involved in water supply in the Enfield area:

Bush Hill Waterworks
This was set up in 1875 by the Bush Hill Park Estate Company to supply the houses it was about to build in the Wellington Road and Village Road area. Problems with the well meant that the supply was at best intermittent and the installation was taken over by the New River Company in 1887. The well was filled in, but the former water tower still survives converted into a private house at Quakers Walk.

Bycullah Waterworks
As with Bush Hill, this was set up to supply a new estate, in this case the prestigious Bycullah Estate, developed from 1879. The waterworks was sited at the cul-de-sac end of Rowantree Road. It was acquired by Enfield Waterworks in 1894 and linked up with its network. It was still functioning as late as 1923, by this time under the control of the Metropolitan Water Board. It was subsequently closed and the site sold off.

East London Waterworks Co.
This company was established by Act of Parliament in 1807 and was essentially an amalgamation of the existing waterworks at Shadwell and West Ham. In 1830 it took over the Hackney Waterworks. In 1893 it was granted powers to build a chain of reservoirs in the Lee Valley and these powers were inherited by the Metropolitan Water Board, when it took over the company in 1904. The Banbury and Lockwood Reservoirs had been completed in 1903. This was followed by the massive King George V Reservoir between Ponders End and Chingford, which opened in 1913. Delayed by the First World War, during which the site was appropriated for an airfield, work eventually began in 1935 on the Girling Reservoir (south of Lea Valley Road). Construction work was halted by the last war and the reservoir was finally opened in 1951. The water is mostly drawn from the Lee, but since 1960 water from the Thames at Hampton has been delivered by a tunnel to the King George V Reservoir.

Three Valleys Water
This company supplies much of the Cockfosters and Hadley Wood areas. It began life as the Barnet District Gas and Water Company, set up by Act of Parliament in 1872. It became the Barnet District Water Company in 1950, after losing the gas side of the business to nationalisation, and in 1960 it merged with the Herts and Essex Water Company to form the Lee Valley Water Company. A subsequent merger resulted in the present organisation.

West Lodge

This substantial property stands on the site of one of the lodges of Enfield Chase. It appears to date mainly from the early 19th century when it was owned by the Paris family, although it is possible that some older work may be concealed behind the white stucco rendering. The house is now a hotel.

164. West Lodge, now a hotel.

Sir Cuthbert Wilfrid Whitaker

The son of Joseph Whitaker *(see below)* and his father's successor as editor of *Whitaker's Almanack*, Whitaker (1873-1950) grew up at White Lodge, Silver Street and moved after his marriage to Elsynge Cottage, Forty Hill. He left Enfield during the First World War and never returned. In 1911 he wrote and published the rather grandiloquently titled *Illustrated Historical, Statistical & Topographical Account of the Urban District of Enfield.*For much of the 20th century this was the most widely read of Enfield histories. From 1965 **Enfield Preservation Society** issued several reprints of the book, giving it an iconic status that, frankly, it does not deserve. It has since been almost completely superseded by David Pam's monumental three volume *History of Enfield* (1990-1994). However, Whitaker's work remains useful where he is writing about people and places that he had known and events that he had witnessed.

Joseph Whitaker

The publisher and editor, Joseph Whitaker (1820-1895), founded *The Bookseller* in 1858. This weekly 'organ' of the book trade, as it used to denote itself on its front cover, is still published today and is widely read by both booksellers and librarians.

In 1868 Whitaker was the founder and first editor of *Whitaker's Almanack*, one of the most useful of all reference books, which has been published annually ever since. In 1862 he moved into White Lodge, a wooden clapboard

165. The King and Tinker near Whitewebbs Lane. The Union Jack at half-mast probably marks the death of King Edward VII, who died in 1910.

166. Whitewebbs, home of the Wilkinson family for over a hundred years.

house that still stands in Silver Street opposite Enfield Civic Centre, where he lived until his death in 1895.

Whitewebbs

A large house built in 1791 for Dr Abraham Wilkinson, whose descendants lived here until 1901. In 1881 the house was altered to a French chateau style. In 1911 the property was acquired by Sir Frederick Orr-Lewis, a wealthy Canadian businessman, who in May 1915 was one of the survivors of the sinking of the *Lusitania*. His son, Sir Duncan Orr-Lewis, sold the property in 1931 to Enfield Council. The grounds are now a public park, part of which is occupied by a golf course, and the house, after being used for many years as an old people's home, has been sold off and is now a restaurant.

Whitewebbs Lane

Known variously as Whitewebbs Lane and Romey Street, originally only the eastern half existed from Bulls Cross to a gate into Enfield Chase close to the King and Tinker pub. The western extension (Whitewebbs Road) was a former track way across The Chase upgraded after the enclosure of 1803.

167. St Mary Magdalene's church (1883) on the summit of Windmill Hill.

Windmill Hill

This was formerly part of East Barnet Road *(see Enfield Road)*, but was known as Windmill Hill by 1851. The name derives from the windmill that stood at the junction of Old Park Road until its demolition in 1904.

Bernie Winters

The popular and much loved comedian Bernie Winters (1932-91) was born, Bernie Weinstein, to a Jewish family in Islington. He worked for many years as a double act with his brother, Mike Winters, and then, after the break up of the partnership, performed solo. He lived for many years in a large house in Cockfosters Road.

Worlds End Lane

A former access road to The Chase. Although the land on either side was in Enfield, prior to boundary adjustments in 1934 the road lay in Southgate (in Edmonton before 1881). As with Botany Bay, the name is clearly an ironic allusion to the then remoteness of the area.

Robert Wroth I

Wroth (1488-1535) lived at **Durants Arbour**, Ponders End. He trained as a lawyer and worked for his powerful and influential neighbour, **Sir Thomas Lovell** of Elsing. In 1529 he was elected to Parliament for Middlesex and in 1531 he was appointed Attorney General to the Duchy of Lancaster. In his will he left a horse to Thomas Cromwell, who also became guardian of Wroth's eighteen-year-old son. The link with Cromwell suggests that the

168. The Enfield Windmill c.1900. It was demolished in 1904.

family was already strongly committed to the Protestant cause.

Robert Wroth II

The grandson of **Robert Wroth I** and son of **Thomas Wroth**, Robert II (1539-1606) shared the political aspirations of his immediate family. His formative years were spent in exile in Strasbourg with his father. He was first elected to Parliament in 1563 for St Albans, a borough constituency under the patronage of the influential Bacon family, and then briefly represented Bossiney in Cornwall. Finally in 1572 he was elected for Middlesex, his father's old seat, which he held without a break until his death. In 1571 he was the principal supporter of an Act for improving the River Lee (*See Lee Navigation*). He was also heavily involved in the passing of the 1601 **Poor Law**, a key piece of legislation, which was to remain at the core of the English poor relief system until 1834.

Thomas Wroth

Son of **Robert Wroth I** of **Durants Arbour**, Wroth (1518-73) was elected for Middlesex in the Parliaments of 1545, 1547, 1559 and 1563. After the fall of the Protector Somerset and his replacement by the Duke of Northumberland, Wroth became one of the gentlemen of the privy chamber to King Edward VI. Shortly before the king's death, Wroth was one of the signatories of letters patent devised to pass the crown to the king's cousin, Lady Jane Grey, thereby bypassing the rightful heir, Mary Tudor, who as a Catholic, was correctly regarded as hostile to the Protestant Reformation. However, when Jane Grey's cause had clearly failed, Wroth, showing remarkable agility, took part in the proclamation of Mary. Despite this *volte face*, his loyalty to the new regime was clearly suspect and in 1554 he took refuge in Strasbourg, a city popular with English Protestant refugees, not returning to England until after Mary's death in 1558. He was again elected to Parliament, but his days of influence were over.

Appendix 1

Enfield Population Figures, 1801/1961 *

1801	5,881	1881	19,104
1811	6,636	1891	31,536
1821	8,227	1901	42,738
1831	8,812	1911	56,338
1841	9,367	1921	60,738
1851	9,453	1931	67,752
1861	12,424	1951	110,465
1871	16,054	1961	109,542

* The pattern of growth has some interesting features: sluggish growth 1821/51, a period of sustained growth 1881/1911, and a period of very rapid growth 1931/1951.

Appendix 2

Other Enfields

Elsewhere in the U.K. there is Enfield, Lancashire, a suburb of Accrington. Its main claim to fame is its cricket team, which was a founder member in 1890 of the North East Lancashire Cricket League. Two years later this organisation formed the core of prestigious Lancashire Cricket League, which survives to this day and has produced many top class players.

In the Irish Republic Enfield, County Meath lies 26 miles west of Dublin and stands on the main road running north-west from Dublin to Mullingar, Carrick On Shannon and Sligo.The village is now normally called Innfield, but the railway station is still called Enfield.

In the USA there are at least five Enfields. The oldest and most substantial of these is Enfield, Connecticut. The settlement was founded in 1680 as an off-shoot of Springfield, Massachusetts and in 1990 had a population of 45, 532. Enfield, Illinois was founded in 1853 in an area which saw its first European settlers as late as 1819. Enfield, New Hampshire is rather older and a more substantial settlement, founded in 1761 by settlers from Connecticut. Enfield, North Carolina is older still, founded in 1740. Elsewhere in North America, Enfield, Nova Scotia lies inland from Halifax.

There are two Enfields in Australia. Enfield, New South Wales is now a suburb of Sydney. Enfield, South Australia, founded in 1839, is now a suburb of Adelaide. There is also an Enfield in New Zealand, a small settlement on South Island, founded in 1876 and believed to have been named after the Enfield rifle.

169. The Old Town Hall in Enfield, Connecticut.

Further Reading

GENERAL WORKS

Victoria County History of Middlesex, Vol. V (1976).
DALLING, Graham, *Enfield Past.* (1999).
HODSON, George & FORD, Edward, *A history of Enfield.* (1873).
PAM, David, *A History of Enfield*. 3 vols. (1990-94).
ROBINSON, William, *The history and antiquities of Enfield.* 2 vols. (1823).
TUFF, John, *Historical topographical and statistical notices of Enfield.* (1858).
WHITAKER, Cuthbert, *An illustrated historical, statistical and topographical account of Enfield.* (1911).

Bush Hill Park
FORD, John Walker, *A sketch towards a history of the neighbourhood: being some particulars of Bush Hill Park.* (1904).
HAIGH, Douglas, *Old Park in the Manor of Enfield.* (1977).
HOY, Denis, *From fields to flats.* (1998).
ROBINSON, Sidney John, *Sid's family Robinson.* (1994).
Enfield Chase
PAM, David, *The story of Enfield Chase.* (1984).
THOMPSON, E.P., *Whigs and hunters: the story of the Black Act.* (1975).
Enfield Town
ENFIELD PRESERVATION SOCIETY, *A portrait of Gentleman's Row.* (1986).
Recollections of old Enfield, first published in the *Enfield Observer.* (1910).
Forty Hill and Bulls Cross
EDWARDS, Jack, *The story of Capel.* (1985).
WILSON, Frances, *Memories of Forty Hill.* (1947).
Hadley Wood
CLARK, Nancy, *Hadley Wood*, 2nd edition. (1978).

BIOGRAPHICAL
John Abernethy
THORNTON, John F., *John Abernethy.* (1953)
Charles Babbage
MOSELEY, Mabeth, *Irascible genius: a life of Charles Babbage, inventor.* (1964).
SWADE, Doran, *The cogwheel brain: Charles Babbage and his quest to build the first computer.* (2000).
Sir Joseph Bazalgette
HALLIDAY, Stephen, *The great stink of London: Sir Joseph Bazalgette and the cleansing of the Victorian capital.* (1999).
Sir John Betjeman
HILLIER, Bevis, *Young Betjeman.* (1988).
WILSON, A. N., *Betjeman.* (1996).
Francis Augustus Bevan
GAMBLE, Audrey Nona, *A history of the Bevan family.* (1924).
Sir John Bland-Sutton
Bett, W.R., *Sir John Bland-Sutton, 1855-1936.* (1956).
William Booth
BEGBIE, Harold, *Life of William Booth.* (1920)
HATTERSLEY, Roy, *Blood and fire: William and Catherine Booth and their Salvation Army.* (1999).
Gussie Bowles
ALLAN, Mea, E.A. *Bowles and his garden at Myddelton House, 1865-1954.* (1973).
HEWITT, Bryan, *The crocus king: E.A. Bowles of Myddelton House.* (1997).
John By
LEGGETT, Robert, *John By: builder of the Rideau Canal: founder of Ottawa.* (1982).
John Cartwright
OSBORNE, John W., *John Cartwright.* (1972).
Charles Cowden Clarke
ALTICK, Richard, *The Cowden Clarkes.* (1948).
CLARKE, Charles Cowden, *Recollections of writers.* (1878).
CLARKE, Mary Cowden, *My long life.* (1896).
Isaac D'Israeli
OGDEN, James, *Isaac D'Israeli* (1969).
Sir Ambrose Fleming
FLEMING, Ambrose, *Memories of a scientific life.* (1934).
MACGREGOR-MORRIS, J. T., *The inventor of the valve.* (1954).
Sir John French
FRENCH, Gerald, *The life of Field-Marshal Sir John French.* (1931).
HOLMES, Richard, *The little Field-Marshal.* (1981).
Sir Nigel Gresley
BROWN, F.A.S., *Nigel Gresley: locomotive engineer.* (1961).
HUGHES, Geoffrey, *Sir Nigel Gresley: the engineer and his family.* (2001).
Radclyffe Hall
CLINE, Sally, *Radclyffe Hall: a woman called John.* (1997).
SOUHAMI, Diana, *The trials of Radclyffe Hall.* (1998).
Thomas Hardy
GITTINGS, Robert, *The older Hardy.* (1978).
GITTINGS, Robert and MANTON, Jo, *The second Mrs Hardy.* (1979).
TOMALIN, Claire, *Thomas Hardy: the time-torn man.* (2006).
Hugh Jenkins
JENKINS, Hugh, *The culture gap.* (1979).
Sir Frederic Wood Jones
CHRISTOPHERS, Barry, 'Frederic Wood Jones at school and at university'. In *Australian & New Zealand Journal of Surgery* (1994), 64, pp.27/37
John Keats
BATE, Walter Jackson, *John Keats.* (1963).
GITTINGS, Robert, *John Keats.* (1968).
MOTION, Andrew, *Keats.* (1997).
WARD, Aileen, *John Keats: the making of a poet.* (1964).
Legh Kilpin
WINTERS, Barbara, *Legh Mulhall Kilpin: teacher: painter: printmaker.* (2003).
Charles Lamb
BURTON, Sarah, *A double-life: a biography of Charles and Mary Lamb.* (2003).
PRANCE, Claude A., *Companion to Charles Lamb.* (1983).
Norman Lewis
LEWIS, Norman, *God bless the squire.* (In *The Happy Ant-Heap*, 1998.)
LEWIS, Norman, *Jackdaw Cake.* (1985).
LEWIS, Norman, *The world, the world.* (1996).
Charles Lightoller
STENSON, Patrick, *Titanic voyager: the odyssey of C.H. Lightoller.* (1998).
Iain Macleod
FISHER, Nigel, *Iain Macleod.* (1973).
SHEPHERD, Robert, *Iain Macleod.* (1994).
Frederick Marryat
POCOCK, Tom, *Captain Marryat: seaman, writer and adventurer.* (2000).
Walter Pater
LEVEY, Michael, *The case of Walter Pater.* (1978)
WRIGHT, Thomas, *The life of Walter Pater.* (1907).
William Pitt the Elder
BLACK, Jeremy, *Pitt the elder.* (1992)
TUNSTALL, Brian. *William Pitt, Earl of Chatham.* (1938).
Max Plowman
PLOWMAN, Max, *A subaltern on the Somme.* (1928).
PLOWMAN, Max, *Bridge into the future: letters of Max Plowman.* (1944).

William Robinson
ABRAHAMS, Aleck, *The life and works of William Robinson.* (1925).
Sir Philip Sassoon
JACKSON, Stanley, *The Sassoons.* (1968).
ROTH, Cecil, *The Sassoon dynasty.* (1941).
STANSKY, Peter, *Sassoon: the world of Philip and Sybil.* (2003).
Sir Osbert Sitwell
SITWELL, Osbert, *The scarlet tree.* (1946).
ZIEGLER, Philip, *Osbert Sitwell.* (1998).
Wroth family
PAM, David, *Protestant gentlemen: the Wroths of Durants Arbour .....* (1973).

AGRARIAN HISTORY
MIDDLETON, John, View of the agriculture of Middlesex. (1778).
BURNBY, J.G.L. & ROBINSON, A.E., *Now turned into fair garden plots.* (1983).

ARCHAEOLOGY
GENTRY, Anne, 'Excavations at Lincoln Road, London Borough of Enfield', November 1974/March 1976. In *LAMAS Trans.* Vol. 28 1977, pp.101/89.
GILLAM, Geoffrey, *Prehistoric and Roman Enfield.* (1973).
IVENS, John, *Finds and excavations in Roman Enfield.* (1977).

ARCHITECTURE
CARTER, Valerie, *Treasures of Enfield.* (2000)
CHERRY, Bridget and PEVSNER, Nikolaus, *London North (Buildings of England).* (1998).
ENFIELD PRESERVATION SOCIETY, *Enfield's architectural heritage.* (1977).
GILLAM, Geoffrey, *Forty Hall, Enfield,* 1629/1997. (1997).
JONES, Ian & DRAYTON, Ivy, *The royal palaces of Enfield.* (1984).
ROYAL COMMISSION ON HISTORICAL MONUMENTS, *An inventory of the historical monuments of Middlesex.* (1937).

CANNING CASE
DE LA TORRE, Lilian, *Elizabeth is missing.* (1947).
MACHEN, Arthur, *The Canning wonder.* (1925).
PHILLIPS, Pauline L., *Upon my word I am no scholar.* (1982).
TREHERNE, John, *The Canning enigma.* (1989).

CONSERVATION
CARTER, Valerie, *Fighting for the future: the story of Enfield Preservation Society,* 1936/1996. (1997).

CO-OPERATIVE MOVEMENT
SMITH, H. Charles, *Co-operation in Enfield and its Environs.* (1932).

EDUCATION
AMBROSE FLEMING SCHOOL, *Ambrose Fleming School Magazine*: special jubilee issue, 1911/1961. (1961)
COLLICOTT, Sylvia, *Enfield School Board.* (1985).
DALLING, Graham, *A history of the Enfield Church School of Industry.* (1989)
FAULKNER, Michael J., *St. Matthew's C. of E. Primary School, 1838-1988.* (1988)
HART, Joan, *Onward ever: the story of Enfield County School for Girls, 1909-1967.* (1999).
HEATHFIELD, John, *A history of Trent C. of E. School, Cockfosters.* (1998).
MARSHALL, Leslie Birkett, *A brief history of Enfield Grammar School.* (1958).
PARKIN, Bernard, *St. Ignatius College, 1894-1994.* (1994).
STEVENSON, Mary, *Remembering Miss M.C. Sharp on the 40th anniversary of her retirement from Enfield County School.* (2002).
STURGES, George W., *Schools of the Edmonton Hundred.* (1949).
TAYLOR, R.W., *A history of a school.* (1968).

HUGUENOTS
COLLINS, William Job, 'The Garnault group of families': In *Huguenot Society Proceedings*, Vol. XIV, no.4.
LEE, Grace Lawless, *The story of the Bosanquets.* (1966).
ROMILLY, Mimi, 'Sir Samuel Romilly of Russell Square and his descendants'. In *Camden History Review*, Vol. 20, pp.5/8.
RONDEAU, Stan, 'Rondeau allegro'. In *Genealogists Magazine*, Vol.27, no.7, pp. 314/5.

INDUSTRY
ENFIELD ARCHAEOLOGICAL SOCIETY, *Industrial archaeology in Enfield.* (1971).
ENFIELD DISTRICT MANUFACTURERS' ASSOCIATION, *Industries of Enfield.* (1947).
LEWIS, Jim, *London's Lea Valley: Britain's best kept secret.* (1999).
LEWIS, Jim, *London's Lea Valley: more secrets revealed.* (2001).

Electrical Manufacturing
BELLING & CO. LTD., *The story of Belling 1911-1962.* (1962)
BELLING-LEE LTD., *Golden jubilee, 1922-1972.* (1972).
EDISWAN LTD., *The pageant of the lamp.* (1949).
Electricity Supply
FRISWELL, Norman, *Northmet: a history of the North Metropolitan Electric Power Supply Co.* (2000)
Firearms
BIRCHMORE, Graham, *The lads of Enfield Lock: 172 years of apprentice training at the Royal Small Arms Factory ... 1816-1988.* (2005).
MINISTRY OF DEFENCE, *British rifles: a catalogue of the Enfield Pattern Room.* (1981).
PAM, David, *The Royal Small Arms Factory, Enfield and its workers.* (1998).
PUTNAM, Tim, *A short history of the Royal Small Arms Factory, Enfield.* (1992).
REYNOLDS, E. G. B., *The Lee-Enfield Rifle.* (1960)
Gas Industry
MERRISON, R.W., *A brief account of the Tottenham and District Gas Company's first hundred years, 1847-1947.* (1947).
TOTTENHAM & DISTRICT GAS GO., *Ponders End Works.* (1949).

PLACE NAMES
DALLING, Graham, *A guide to Enfield street names.* (1982).
ENGLISH PLACE-NAMES SOCIETY, *The place-names of Middlesex.* (1942)
FIELD, John, *Place names of Greater London.* (1980)

POLICE
KENNISON, Peter, *Behind the blue lamp: policing North and East London.* (2003).

POOR LAW
GRAHAM, Margaret, *The Chase Farm Schools.* (1974).
NEECH, Henry C., *Chase Farm Schools: a good start for a boy: my life story 1905-1965.* (1998).
RICHARDSON, Stanley I., *A history of the Edmonton Poor Law Union 1837-1854.* (1968).

PUBLIC HOUSES
BOUDIER, Gary, *A-Z of Enfield pubs: part 1: Eastern and Western Enfield plus Monken Hadley.* (2000).

STANDBROOK, Stanley W., *Fifty years plus 1924/1974: a family in the licensed trade.* (1997).

RELIGION

MUDIE-SMITH, Richard, *The religious life of London.* (1904).

Roman Catholicism

AVERY, David, *Popish recusancy in the Elizabethan Hundred of Edmonton.* (1968).

WORRALL, Edward S. *The Confessor William Le Hunt: priest and schoolmaster.* (1962).

Church of England

LONDON & MIDDLESEX ARCHAEOLOGICAL SOCIETY, *Middlesex parish churches.* (1955).

SPERLING, John Hanson, *Church walks in Middlesex.* (1849).

Nonconformity

KNIGHT, Geoffrey, *Nonconformist churches in Enfield.* (1973).

SEWERAGE

MIDDLESEX COUNTY COUNCIL, *Report on sewerage and main drainage in East Middlesex.* (1936).

MIDDLESEX COUNTY COUNCIL, *Inauguration of the East Middlesex main drainage undertaking.* (1957).

SPORT

Bowls

WALKER, Patsy, *The history of Enfield Bowling Club: the first twenty-five years.* (1991).

WALKER, Patsy, *Enfield Bowling Club: forty more years 1950-1991.* (1992).

Cricket

COCKFOSTERS CRICKET CLUB, *Cockfosters Cricket Club: a history of the first hundred years.* (1973).

COLLINS, Steve, *Botany Bay: a century of village cricket.* (1999).

COLLINS, Steve, *Enfield Cricket Club: 150 years not out.* (2006).

NORTH ENFIELD CRICKET CLUB, *One hundred years to remember: a history of North Enfield Cricket Club, 1886-1996.* (1986).

Football

DIMENT, Alan, *Simply the E's: a history of Enfield Football Club.* (2006).

Golf

BROWN, Vivian Maxwell, *A brief history of Bush Hill Park Golf Club.* (1997).

DICKINSON, Bill, *Enfield Golf Club: a centenary history, 1893-1993.* (1994).

TAYLOR, Pat, *Hadley Wood: the story of a golf club, 1922-1997.* (1997).

TODD, Andrew, *Crews Hill: the story of a golf club, 1915-1991.* (1991).

Rugby

PERRY, Haydn, *Saracens Football Club (R.F.U.), 1876-1976.* (1976).

THEATRES & CINEMAS

GILLAM, Geoffrey, *Theatres, music halls and cinemas in the London Borough of Enfield.* (1986).

TRADE UNIONS

AMALGAMATED UNION OF ENGINEERS & FOUNDRY WORKERS, *Some account to 1935 of the Enfield Lock Branch.* (1970).

TRANSPORT

General Works

BARKER, T. E. and ROBBINS, Michael, *A history of London Transport.* 2 vols. (1963/74).

SEKON, G. A., *Locomotion in Victorian London.* (1938).

Buses

BLACKER, K. C. and others, *London's buses: Vol.1: the independent era, 1922-1934.* (1977).

Railways

BROWN, Joe, *London railway atlas.* (2006).

CROOME, Desmond and JACKSON, Alan, *Rails through the Clay.* (1993).

GLOVER, John, *Eastern electric.* (2003).

HALLIDAY, Stephen, *Underground to everywhere.* (2004).

JACKSON, Alan, *London's local railways.* (1999).

WHITE, H. P., *A regional history of the railways of Great Britain: Vol.3: Greater London.* (1987).

Great Eastern

ALLEN, Cecil, J., *The Great Eastern Railway.* (1968).

CONNOR, Jim, *Branch lines to Enfield Town and Palace Gates.* (2004).

HILL, Jim, *Buckjumpers, gobblers and clauds: a lifetime on Great Eastern and LNER footplates.* (1981).

Great Northern

HODGE, Peter, *The Hertford Loop.* (1976).

WROTTESLEY, John, *The Great Northern Railway.* 3 vols. (1979/81).

YOUNG, John, *Great Northern Suburban.* (1977).

Piccadilly Line

CROOME, Desmond, *The Piccadilly Line.* (1998).

LEE, Charles E., *Sixty years of the Piccadilly.* (1966).

Roads

PAM, David, *The Stamford Hill and Green Lanes Turnpike Trust.* 2 vols. (1963/4).

Tramways

HARLEY, Robert J., *Waltham Cross and Edmonton tramways.* (1998).

JONES, Dave, *Enfield and Wood Green tramways.* (1997).

SMEETON, Cyril S. *The Metropolitan Electric Tramways.* 2 vols. (1984/6).

Waterways

DENNEY, Martin, *London's waterways.* (1977).

BURNBY, J.G.L. and PARKER, M. *The Navigation of the River Lee, 1190-1790.* (1978).

WAR

ENFIELD URBAN DISTRICT COUNCIL, *Enfield Victory Celebrations, 8 June 1946.* (1946).

GILLAM, Geoffrey, *Enfield at war 1914-1918.* (1982).

GILLAM, Geoffrey, *Enfield at war 1939-1945.* (1985).

PLUCKWELL, *George, Children of the war.* (1966).

WATER SUPPLY

BARRY, Septimus, *Some notes concerning the growth and development of water supply and storage in Chingford.* (1975).

DICKINSON, H. W., *Water supply of Greater London.* (1954).

ESSEX-LOPRESTI, Michael, *Exploring the New River.* (1986).

GOUGH, J. W., *Sir Hugh Myddelton, entrepreneur and engineer.* (1964).

METROPOLITAN WATER BOARD, *Chingford Reservoir: inauguration by King George V.* (1913).

WARD, Robert, *London's New River.* (2003).

Index

Asterisks denote illustration or caption

A10 *see* Great Cambridge Road
Abbey Road 18
ABC cinema 27
Abercrombie, Sir Patrick 69
Abernethy, John 6, *6
Adath Yisrael Cemetery 22
Adelaide House, Forty Hill 16, *107, 108
Admiral buses 16
Albany Estate 35
Albany Park 77
Albany Pool 102
Albany School 99
All Saints, Edmonton 6, 62, 71, 72
Allom, Sir Charles 50
Alma Road 35, 83, 84, 95, 97
Alma Road Pumping Station *108, 109
Alma School 98
Ambrose Fleming School 99
Angel Road 93
Angel Road station 41
Ansell's Green 73
Applin, Lt. Col. Reginald 6-7, *6
Archaeology 17, 36, 84-5
Archway House 48, *48
Archway Road/Place 48
Archway Tavern 48
Armstrong, Edmund 45
Asbury, Jacob Vale 7, *7
Avenues, The 17, 96
Ayley Croft Lane 67

BABBAGE, Charles 7, 72
Bagsot Road 18
Bailey's Field 44
Baker Street 6, 7, *7, 33, 44, 47, 60, 72, 73, 90, 99
Baptists and their churches 7-8, *8
Barclays Bank 10, 29, *41
Barnet, Battle of 28
Barnet District Gas and Water Co. 109
Barnet General Hospital 56
Bartrams Lane, Hadley Wood 10
Basevi, George 33
Bay Cottage, Church Street 62
Bazalgette, Sir Joseph 8, *8, 32
Beacon of Light Spiritualist Church 64
Bean, Sir Timothy 10
Beauchamp House *75
Beech Hill 9, 108
Beech Hill Park and Estate 9, 28, 29, 30, 108
Bell, Adrian 9
Bell, Sir Martin 9
Bell Lane 9, 35
Belling 59
Belling-Lee 59
Bennett, A T 16
Berry, Sir Anthony 9, *9
Betjeman, Sir John 9-10
Bevan family 10, 29, 31, 97, 103
Birkbeck Estate 43
Bishop Stopford School 98
Bland-Sutton, Sir John 10
Blishen, Edward 10
Boddam, Rawson Hart 19
Bohun Gate 21
Booth, Bramwell 10
Booth, William 10, *10
Bosanquet family 11, *11, 28, 31, 57, 58
Botany Bay 11
Botany Bay Cricket Club 31
Botany Bay School 98-9
Boundary Ditch 93
Bowles, Edward Augustus 11-12, *11, 65, 73, *74, 79
Bowles, Sir Henry 11, 12, *12, 45, 65
Bowles Henry Carrington 45, 65, 73
Bowling Green House 58
Boxers Lake 93
Boys' Brigade 80, 81
Bramley family 41
Bramley Road 41, 66, 95
Branch, James 12
Braughing 96
Bressey, Sir Charles 69
Brick Kiln Lane 67
Brick Lane 12
Brickfield Lane 67
Brickmaking 35, 58
Bridge Street 28, 46
Bridgen Hall Estate 47
Bridgenhall Road 47
Brigadier Hill 12, *13
Brigadier House 12, 13
Brimsdown 12
Brimsdown Power Station 12, *13
Brimsdown School 99
Brimsdown station 12, 34, 85, *85
British Aerospace 96
British Waterways Board 64
Brooklyn, Private Road 71
Browning Road 12, 13
Bull, Bartle 13
Bulls Cross 11, 14, *14, 48, 58, 79
Bulls Cross Lane 46
Bulls Cross Ride 22
Bullsmoor Lane 5, 17, 19, 73
Bullsmoor School 99
Bungey Lane 67
Burleigh Road 95
Burleigh Way 27
Bury Street 85, 94
Buses 14-17, *15, 49, 85, 105, *105
Bush Hill Park Golf Club 19, 45, *76, 77, 85
Bush Hill Park House and Estate 17-18, *18, 19, 36, 72, 95, 106, 109
Bush Hill Park Library 18, 65
Bush Hill Park Methodist Church 73
Bush Hill Park Recreation Ground 77
Bush Hill Park School 18, 98
Bush Hill Park station 87
Bush Hill Waterworks 109
By, John *18, 19, 96
Bycullah Estate 43, 80, 109
Bycullah Waterworks 109

CAMLET HOUSE, Hadley Wood 50
Camlet Moat 9
Camlet Way 9
Canning, Elizabeth 19, *19
Canon cinema 27
Capel House 19-20, *20, 47
Capel Manor Horticultural College 79
Capel Manor School 47, 99
Cardigan Estate 17
Carisbrook Close 75
Carlile, Richard 20
Carlton House, Baker Street 33, 60, 90, 92
Carnegie Trust 65
Carter, Valerie 40
Carterhatch Lane 20, *20, 35, 64, 87
Carterhatch School 99, *99
Cartwright, John 20-1, *20
Case, Charles 16
Cat Hill 21
Cathale Priory 21
Cattlegate Lane 35
Cattlegate Road 21
Cecil Road 7, *8, 43, 65, 72, 95, 98
Cedar Road 79
Cedars Estate 43
Cemeteries 21-2, 94
Cemetery Road 79
Central Library 65, *65, *66
Chalk Farm, Camden 22
Chalk Lane 22, *22, 31
Chambers, Charles 39
Chapel Street 22, 93
Chase Boys' School 39, 99
Chase Farm Hospital 55-6, *56, 84
Chase Farm School 55, 84
Chase Girls' School 99
Chase Green 31, 40, 75, 88
Chase Green Avenue *23
Chase Hill 20, 79
Chase Lane 50
Chase Lodge, Holtwhites Hill *55
Chase Side 23, *23, 30, 59, 61, 73, 87, 93, 97
Chase Side Crescent 57
Chase Side House 23-4, *24
Chase Side School 59, 98
Cheshunt 5, 84, 96
Chesterfield Road School 26, 98, *98
Chine, The 49, 93
Cholera 22, 103
Christ Church, Cockfosters 10, 24, 25, 29, 103
Christ Church Congregational Church. Chase Side 59, 80, 81, 90, 102, 106, *107
Church Lane 24, *24
Church of Christ the King 95
Church Street, Edmonton 60, 62
Church Street, Enfield *25, 26, 39, 93
Churchbury Field 26
Churchbury House, Churchbury Lane *25
Churchbury Lane *25, 26, 44, 75
Churchbury station 87
Cinemas *26, 27
Cineworld, Southbury Road 27
Clarendon Cottage, Gentleman's Row 61
Clarke, Charles Cowden 21, 27-8, *27, 60
Clarke, John 27, *27, 33, 60
Clarke, Mary 27-8
Clay Hill 11, *27
Clayesmore 11, 28, *28, 57, 58
Clayton family 77
Coaches 14-17, 34, 81
Cock, The, Chalk Lane 29
Cockfosters 28-9
Cockfosters Cricket Club 31
Cockfosters Road 30, 111
Cocksmiths End 3431,
College Court 106
Comreddy Gutter 94
Cooper's Lane Road 30-1
Co-operative Movement 30
Cottage, The, Games Road 66
Cranfield family 35
Crescent East 10, 29
Crescent Road 77
Crescent West 29
Cresswell, Daniel 51
Crew, William 31
Crews Hill 31, *31, 59
Crews Hill station 31, 47, 88
Cricket 31
Cromwell, Thomas 111
Cuffley 88
Cuffley Brook 73, 94
Culloden Road 80

D'AGUILA, Hanamel 60

D'Israeli, Benjamin 60
D'Israeli, Isaac 33, *33
Da Costa, Aaron 60
Da Costa, Benjamin Mendes 60
Daisley, Geoffrey 40
Danish invasion 62
Davies, Ernest 13, 31-2, 53
De Bohun family 37, 39
De Bohun Library 66
De Mandeville family 36-7, 39
Dent, J M 32, *32
Derby Road 83
Devine, Alex 28
Dickens, Alfred 109
Distin, Dr Howard *58
Domesday Survey 41, 97
Dower House, Forty Hill 90
Drayton, Ivy 36
Duck Lees Lane 33-4
Dugdale, Edward *98
Dugdale, Florence Emily 51
Dunraven, The Ridgeway 102
Durants Arbour *33, 111
Durants Park 77, *78
Durants Road 83, 98

EAGLE HOUSE, Ponders End 109
Eagles, Edwin Mortimer *38
East Barnet Road 41
East Enfield 34
East Field 9
East Lodge 35
East Lodge Lane 35
East London Waterworks Co. 109
Eastbury Avenue 73
Eastfield School 98
Edenbridge Road 18
Ediswan 83
Edmonton 5, 39, 84
Edmonton Board of Guardians 55, 57, 67, 84
Edmonton Council 57
Edmonton Green 85, 94
Edmonton Green Shopping Centre 66
Edmonton Hundred 5
Edmonton Hundred Historical Society 35-6
Edmonton Library 66
Edmonton Poor Law Union 5, 84
Edmonton Road 54
Edmonton Union Workhouse 57, 84
Edmonton Workmen's Train Association 87
Edward VI, King 46
Electric Theatre, Ponders End *26, 27
Elizabeth, I, Queen 46
Elms, The, Forty Hill 11
Elsing House and Estate 35, 36, 46, 69
Elsynge Cottage 110
Emery, James 39
Enfield, London Borough of 65, 68, 77
Enfield Advertiser 68
Enfield Amateur Cricket Club 31
Enfield and St Albans Co-op 30
Enfield Archaeological Society 35, 36, 46
Enfield Baptist Church *8
Enfield Board of Health 65, 67, 93, 101, 103, 109
Enfield Borough Council 24, 27, 44, 67-8, *68, 111
Enfield British School 97
Enfield Burial Board 21-22
Enfield Central School 99
Enfield Chase 9,20, 21, 23, 28, 30, 31, 35, 36-7, *36, 41, 48, 55, 62, 76, 79, 93. 102, 108, 109, 111
Enfield Chase station 41, 88
Enfield Chronicle 68
Enfield Cottage Hospital 92
Enfield County School 79, 99
Enfield Court 37, *37, 100
Enfield Cricket Club 31, 48
Enfield Education Committee 102
Enfield Empire 27
Enfield Football Club 44-5, *45
Enfield Gazette 68
Enfield Golf Club 77
Enfield Grammar School 37, *37, *38, 39, *39, 59, 60, 64, 79, 93, 99
Enfield Highway 5, 10, 20, 22, 34, 54, 60, 81, *82
Enfield Highway Co-operative Society 30, 35, 96
Enfield Highway Library 65, *65
Enfield Independent 68
Enfield Island Village 19, 96
Enfield Isolation Hospital 57, 90-92
Enfield Lock station 34
Enfield Manor House 39-40, *40
Enfield markets 41
Enfield Methodist Church 106
Enfield New Town 43
Enfield Palace 39
Enfield Post 68
Enfield Preservation Society 40, 110
Enfield Road 41, 65, 66
Enfield School Board 18, 67, 90, 98-99, 102
Enfield Town 41, *42, 68
Enfield Town Constitutional Club 39
Enfield Town Co-operative Society 30
Enfield Town FC 45
Enfield Town station 41, 60, 85, 87, 88, *88
Enfield Urban District Council 22, 40, 57, 67
Enfield Vestry 67
Enfield Wash 5, 34, *35, 54, 60
Enfield Waterworks 109
Enfield Weekly Herald 68
Enfield Workhouse 7, 84
Ensign Buses 16
Ermine Street 14, 44, 67, 95-6
Essex Road 43
Everett, Denton 79

FALLOW BUCK pub 31
Faversham Avenue 18
Fermor-Hesketh, Thomas 44
Fighting Cocks Lane 49
Filcaps Farm and Lane 50
First World War 16, 47-8, 57, 83, 96
Flash Lane 73, 94
Fleming, Sir Ambrose 44
Flooding 92, 93
Folkestone, Viscount 44
Ford, Edward 45, 55, 77
Ford, John Walker 77
Ford, William Frederick 32
Forty Hall and Estate and Park 12, 36, 45, *45, *46, 47, 77, 90, 94
Forty Hill 11, 12, 16, 46, *46
Forty Hill School 64, 97
Forty Hill station 87
Freeman, Rev. Stephen, academy 7, 72
Freezywater 5, 35, 54
French, Gerald 48
French, Sir John 47-8
Freston Gardens 106

GAMES ROAD 66
Garnault family 58, 73
Garnault, Bulls Cross 11
Garnault Road 47
Gater family 59
Genotin Road 27
Gentleman's Row 48, *48, *49, 61, 65
George Spicer School 98, 99, 102
Gillam, Geoffrey 36
Girling Reservoir 109
Gladbeck Way *86, 88
Glebe estate 43
Glover family 15-16
Glover's omnibus 85
Goat, The 46, 48
Goat Lane 48, *49, 75
Godfrey, Dr Benjamin 90
Goldberg, David 60
Golden Hive, Brimsdown 12, *13
Goldsdown Road 48
Gordon Hill 59
Gordon Hill station 47, 88
Gordon House 49
Gordon House Estate 43
Gordon Road 49, 98
Gough Park and Estate 47, 73
Gowland, James 55
Granada, Burleigh Way 27
Grange Drive 49
Grange Park 49, 93
Grange Park School 99
Grange Park station 49, 88
Grangeway, The 49
Gravel digging 58-9
Great Cambridge Road 5, 18, 47, 49-50, *49-50, 59, 83, 94
Great Eastern Railway 12, 16, 17, 34, 41, 43, 81, 85, 87
Great Northern Railway 29, 31, 41, 43, 79, 87-8
Greater London Council 30, 68, 77
Green Belt 30, 31, 43, 47
Green Dragon Lane 16, 49, 50
Green Dragon pub 50, *104
Green Lanes 50
Green Line buses 17
Green Road 66
Green Street 10, 12, *13, 34, 35, 81
Greenwood, Anthony 40
Greenwood, Hadley Wood 29
Gresley, Sir Nigel 50, *50
Greyhound Inn 28, *41
Greystoke Gardens 101
Grout and Baylis crape factory 83
Grove House 60
Grove Road 35

HADLEY COMMON 28
Hadley Road 93
Hadley Wood 10, 28-9
Hadley Wood Golf Club 50, 108
Hadley Wood School 99
Hadley Wood station 30
Halcyon House, Private Road 71
Halifax Road *23
Hall, Radclyffe 50-1, *51
Hammond, Thomas 60
Hardy, Thomas 51, *98
Harman, Edward 28
Hawkes, Christopher 55
Hawkes, Jacquetta 55
Heath, Rev. John Moore 24, 39, 51-2, *51, 70, 97, 108
Heddon Court 29, 30
Heddon Court Avenue 10
Heddon Court School 9, 10
Henderson, Arthur *51, 53
Henderson, William 6, 31, 44, *51, 52-4
Henry IV, King 37
Hertford Road 5, 9, 15, 19, 27, 34, *34, 35, *35, 54, *54, 65, 81, 87, 94, 97
Hertford Union Canal 64
High Street, Ponders End 54, *54, 73, 81, 83, *83, 109
Highlands Hospital 56-7, *56
Highlands School 99
Highlands Village 56
Hill Lodge, Clay Hill 8, 32
Hilly Fields 47, 77, 94

Hodson, George Hewitt 45, 54-5, *55, 97
Hodson, William 55
Hoe Lane 35, 55
Holly Bush pub 23
Holly Bush School 97
Holly Walk 15, 40, 93
Holmes, Richard 48
Holmwood, Baker Street 7, 72
Holtwhites Hill 55, *55
Holtwhites Hill reservoir 109
Holy Family Convent School 98
Honilands school 99
Hopkins, Sir Frederick Gowland 55
Hornsey 5, 84
Horsepoolstones 34
Horseshoe Lane 27
Hospitals 55-58, *56-58
Houndsden Gutter 93
Houndsfield Road Library 66
Howard, Sir Seymour 68
Huguenots 58
Hume, Mrs Ann 28

INDUSTRY 58-9, *59, 83
Insanitary areas 83

JACK, Charles 29
Jebb, Richard 29
Jenkins, Hugh *38, 59, 64
Jenkins, Joseph 59
Jeremy Green's Lane 85
Jesus Church, Forty Hill 12, 24, *24, 47
Jews in Enfield 22, 60
Joan Potter's Lane 67
Jolly Farmers pub 41
Jones, Sir Frederic Wood 60
Jones, Ian 36
Jubilee Hall, Parsonage Lane 40
Jute mill 83

KARLOFF, Boris 60
Keats, John 60, *61, 127
Kempe Road Library 65
Kilpin, Legh 60
Kilvington Hall School 76
King & Tinker 46, *110, 111
King George V Reservoir 109
King George Playing field 77
King's Head 15
Kingdom, Cornelia 12
Kingsmead School 99
Kronman, Philip 60

LAKESIDE 80, 101
Lamb, Charles 7, 27, 61-2, *61
Lamb, Mary 61, *61
Lancaster, Duchy of 29, 37, 39, 62
Lancaster Avenue 10, 29
Lancaster Road 16, 23, 59, 62, 64, 87, 106
Landseer Road 95
Lane, Carinthia Arbuthnot 40
Latymer Road 94
Lavender Fields 62
Lavender Hill 62
Lavender Hill Cemetery 22, *22, 94
Lavender School 98
Layard Road 47
Lazarus, A 60
Lea Valley Road 62, 73, 81, 84, 101
Lee, River 35, 62, *63, 64, 75, 92, *92, 109
Lee Conservancy Board 64, 92
Lee Marshes 35
Lee Navigation 62, *63, 64, 83, 112
Lee Valley Water Co. 109
Leeging Beech Gutter 93
Lewis, Frederick 108
Lewis, Norman 12, 59, 64-5
Lewis, Richard 64
Lewis, Rev. T Winchester 45, 77
Libraries 65-6, *65-6
Library Green 23, 24, 40
Lightoller, Charles 66
Lilburn Lodge 55
Lincoln House Estate 83
Lincoln Road 17, 31, 44, 57, 67, *67, 83, 85
Little Woodside 23
Local Government 67-8
Lochnagar, Rowantree Road 80
Lock Lane 77
Locks, 62, *63, 64, *64
London & North Eastern Railway 87, 88
London County Council 56, 67
London General Omnibus Co. 16
London Passenger Transport Board 104
London Public Omnibus Co. 16
London Road 7, *8, 43, 69, *69, 81, 93, 94, *95
Longbourn, Forty Hill 11
Lonsdale Drive 80, 101
Love's Row 22
Lovell, Sir Thomas 46, 69, 97, 111
Lower Water Lane 48
Ludgrove, Hadley Wood 30
Ludgrove School, Cockfosters 99

M25 5, 47, 69, *69, 92
Mackie, John 32, 70, *70
Mackmurdo, Arthu Heygate 71
Maclagan, William Dalrymple 52, 70, *70
Macleod, Iain 59, 71, *71
Magee, Patrick 9
Maidens Bridge *15, 94
Maidens Brook 94, *94
Main Avenue 18, 106
Mallard locomotive 50, *50
Mandeville Road 35
Manners, Thomas, Earl of Rutland 69
Manor House, Bulls Cross 47, 58, 60
Market Cross *43, *74
Market gardening 31, 35, 43, 59
Market Place *43
Marryat, Frederick 7, 72, *72
Marsh Lane 77
Medcalf Road 35
Mellish, William 17, 72, *72
Merrybills Brook 93
Merryhills Drive 101
Merryhills Library, Enfield Road 65, 66
Merryhills School 99
Metherell, Richard 49
Methodists 72-3
Metropolitan Asylums Board 56
Metropolitan Electric Tramways 104
Metropolitan Water Board 109
Meyer family 45, *45, 47
Meyers, John Henry 68
Michell, Matthew 60
Middlesex County Council 30, 37, 55-6, 57, 67, 68, 76, 84
Middlesex Polytechnic 30
Millfield Theatre 66
Millmarsh Lane 35, 73
Milne, Rev. John 37, 39
Monastery Gardens 79, 90, *91
Monken Hadley 5, 28, 37
Monkey Mead Brook 93
Montagu Road 22, 85
Moorhatch Gate Street 102
Myddelton, Sir Hugh 73
Myddelton Avenue 47
Myddelton House 11-12, *11, 47, 58, 73, *73, *74

NAG'S HEAD LANE *see* Southbury Road
Nag's Head Road 62, 73, 83, 101
Napier Road 83
Naylor, Louise 60
New Lane 62
New Lane Road 62
New River 46-7, 58, 73, 75-6, *75, 93, 109
New River Estate 18
Newman, John Pretyman 12, 76
Newspapers 68, *69
Norgrove, Uplands Park Road 60
North Circular Road 5
North Enfield Cricket Club 31
North Enfield Recreation Ground 47, 77
North Lodge 76
North London Suburban Tramways Co. 103
North Metropolitan Electric Power Supply. Co. 12
North Metropolitan Tramways Co. 104
North Middlesex Hospital 57, 84
Northern Isolation Hospital 56
North-South road 76-7
Novello family 27

OAK HOUSE 81
Oakwood Library 66
Old Enfield Charitable Trust 81
Old Park and Estate 19, 43, 45, 49, *76, 77, 85
Old Park Avenue 39, 106
Old Park Farm 77
Old Park Grange Estate 88
Old Park Lane 50
Old Park Ridings 49, 93
Old Park Road 77, 112
Oldbury Lane 101
Orchard Way 44
Ordnance Factory Lane 77
Ordnance Factory station 85
Ordnance Road 35, 77, *77
Ordnance Road School 97
Orr-Lewis, Sir Duncan 47, 111
Orr-Lewis, Sir Frederick 111

PALACE GARDENS Precinct 44, 77
Palmers Green 12, 16
Pam, David 36, 40
Paris family 109, *110
Park Avenue 18
Parker Bowles family 45, 58
Parks and open spaces 47, 77
Parliamentary representation 6-7, 9, 12, 13, 31-2, 44, 53, 59, 70, 71, 76, 78-9
Parsonage Lane 40, 79, *79, 90, 93
Parsonage Lane Road 55
Pater, Walter 79
Peace Pledge Union 81
Perkins family 16
Perry, Frances 79
Perry's Hardy Plant Farm 79
Phipps Hatch Lane 12, 79, *80
Piccadilly Line 43, 89, *89
Picturedrome 27
Pied Bull, Bulls Cross *14, 79
Pigots Lane 35
Pitt, William the elder 79-80, *80, 101
Pleydell-Bouverie, William 44
Plough, Crews Hill *31
Plough, Turkey Street *106
Plowman, Max 80-1, *81
Plowman, Tom 80
Policing and police stations 81, *81
Ponders End 5, 16, 81, *82, 83, *83
Ponders End Congregatioinal Church 106
Ponders End Electric Theatre *26, 27
Ponders End Library 65
Ponders End Lock *64
Ponders End Methodist Church 73
Ponders End Mill 58, 83
Ponders End Recreation Ground 77
Ponders End Shell Works 83
Ponders End station 41, 84, 85, *86
Poor Law 84

Poplars, The, Chase Side 61, *61
Potters Bar 5
Potters Bar Road 92
Prehistoric Enfield 84-5
Premier cinema, Hertford Road 27
Priestley, J B 55
Primitive Methodists 18, 73
Prince of Wales School 99
Private Road, Bush Hill Park 60, 71
Public Libraries 18, 65-6, *65-6
Putney Lodge Estate 35
Pymmes Brook 88, 93

QUAKERS WALK 109
Queen's Hall cinema *26, 27

RAILWAYS 85, *85-6, 87-9, *88-9
Rainton, Sir Nicholas 45, 89-90, *90, 97
Raleigh Road 43
Rectory Manor House 79, 90, *91
Red Lane 67, 85
Redburn's *15, 16, *16
Reddaford, Slades Hill 100
Registry Office 65
Rendlesham Viaduct 94
Rhys, Ernest 32
Rialto cinema, Burleigh Way 27
Ridewood, William 39
Ridge, Dr John James 57, 90, *90, 92
Ridge Avenue 93
Ridgeway, The 11, 35, 55, 60, 92, *92, 102
River Front 51
Robinson, William 94
Roman Catholics and churches 95, *95
Romans in Enfield 17, 95-6
Romey Street 46, 111
Rondeau, James 58
Rose and Crown 28, 46
Rosemary Avenue 6
Rowantree Road 80, 109
Royal Small Arms Factory 12, *18, 19, 26, 30, 35, 59, 64, 77, 96, *96
Russell, Francis 28
Russell Road 47
Rutland, Earl of 69
Ryland, Rev. John 27

SACKVILLE-WEST, Edward 101
Saddlers Mill Stream 93
St Andrew's Church 6, *21, 24, 37, 40, 41, 51-2, *52, 54, 60, 70, 90, 97, *97, 108
St Andrew's School 51, 97, *98
St Anne's School 98
St George's Church, Freezywater 25
St George's Road 47
St George's School 97
St Giles' Church, Bullsmoor Lane 26
St Ignatius School 98
St James' Church, Enfield Highway 24, *34, 35, 83
St James' School 10, 76, 97
St John's Church, Clay Hill *25
St John's School 76, 97
St Luke's Church, Browning Road 12, 13, 25
St Mark's Church, Bush Hill Park 18, 24
St Mark's School 18, 65
St Mary Magdalene, Windmill Hill 23, 24, *111
St Mary's Church, Nags Head Road 95
St Mary's RC school 97
St Matthew's, Ponders End 24, 83
St Matthew's School 97
St Michael and all Angels, Gordon Hill 24
St Michael's Hospital 57
St Nicholas House 76
St Paul's Presbyterian Church 72, 106
St Paul's Church, Hadley Wood 25
St Peter and St Paul, Ordnance Road 25-6
St Peter's Church, Grange Park 26
St Stephen's Church, Bush hill Park 18, 45
Salmons Brook 75, 88, 93, *93
Salvation Army 10, 73
Sassoon, Sir Edward 30
Sassoon, Sir Philip *29, 30, 97, 99-100
Savoy cinema, Southbury Road 27
Saxons 62
Schools 27, 28, 30, 33, 54-5, 72, 76, 97-99
Scotland Green 81, 83
Scotland Green Road 99
Second World War 18, 24, 26, 30, 37, 56, *83, 96, *105
Sewage works 93
Silver Street 7, 27, 66, 75, 81, 84, 99, *100, 110, 111
Sittingbourne Avenue 18
Sitwell, Sir Osbert 99-100
Skinner, John Bruce 44
Slade family 41
Slades Hill 41, 93, 100
Smeaton, John 64
Smith, Irene 41
Somerset, Col. Sir Alfred 37, *37, 100, *100
Soper, Eileen 100-101
South Lodge 80, 101, *101
South Lodge Hospital 57, *57, 92
South Mimms 5, 37
South Street 73, 81, 83, *83, 101, *101
Southbury Road *(formerly Nag's Head Lane)* 16, 27, *27, 41, 44, *45, 64, 75, 81, 85, 101, 102, *102, 109
Southbury School 98
Southbury station 87
Southgate 16
Southgate Borough Council 31
Southgate High Street Library 65
Southgate Road 30
Spicer, George 90, 102, *102
Stagg Hill 30
Stamford Hill and Green Lanes Turnpike Trust 54, 69
Sterling Way 57
Stockingswater Lane 35
Stort, River 64
Strayfield Road 31, 102
Stringer, William 34
Suffolks Baptist Church 8
Suffolks Estate 35
Suffolks School 98, 99
Swimming Pools 102-103, *102
Sydney Road 43, 51, 64
Synagogues 60

TABOR, Robert Stammers 103
Tenniswood Road 75, 92
Thames Water 109
Theobalds Grove station 87
Theobalds Park Road 103
Thorn's 59
Thornton, Henry 87
Three Valleys Water 109
Tiptoft, Joyce 97
Tottenham 5, 84
Totteridge Road 35
Totteridge Road Baptist Church 8
Town Park 24, 75, 77, *78, 93
Trams 18, 34-5, 81, 87, 103-104, *104
Trent National School 103
Trent Park (house and estate) 10, 28, *28, 29, *29, 30, 31, 93, 97, 100
Trent Park (park) 77
Trinity Church 72, *72
Trolleybuses 35, 43, 81, 83, 105, *105
Tucker, Mr 44
Tucker's Field 47
Tuff, John 105-106, *105-106
Tufnell, Jo 9
Turkey Brook 34, 73, 94, *94
Turkey Street 34, 73, 94, *94, 106, *106
Turkey Street station 47, 87
Twells, Philip 23
Two Brewers pub *83

UNITED Flexible Metal Tubing 59, *59, 83
United Reformed Church 18, 72, *72, 81, 83, 106
University of Middlesex 30
Uplands Park Road 9, 55, 60
Uvedale, Dr Robert 39
Uvedale Cottage, Holly Walk 15
Uvedale Road 93

VESTRY HOUSE 81
Vicars Moor Lane 50
Village Road 17, 18, 93, 109
Vine, The 41

WADDINGTON, David 52, 97, 106-108, *107
Wagon Road 29, 108
Waltham, Abbot of 62
Waltham Abbey 5, 62, 84
Waltham Cross 5
Waltham Lock *63
Waltham Road 54
War Memorial Hospital 57-8, *57, *58
Ware Road 54
Warren family 20
Warwick, Walter Curry 108, *108
Warwick Road 35
Watch house 81
Water Lane 48, 85
Water Lane station 41
Water supplies 109
Waugh, Evelyn 10
Waverley Road 77
Weir Hall Library 66
Welches Lane 77
Wellington Road 17, *17, 60, 93, 109
West Lodge, Hadley Wood 28, 29, 109
Western Synagogue 22
Westpole Farm 30, 41
Westwood, Thomas 61
Westwood Cottage 61, *61
Wharf Road 83
Whitaker, Sir Cuthbert 110
Whitaker, Joseph 110-111
White, Thomas Holt 55, *55
White Horse, Brimsdown 12, *13
White Lodge, Silver Street 7, 110-111
Whitewebbs and Estate 46, 47, 73, 111, *111
Whitewebbs Golf Course 73, 94
Whitewebbs Lane 46, 48, 94, *110, 111
Whitewebbs Recreation Ground 77
Whitewebbs Road 111
Wildwoods 58, 94
Wilkinson family 47, 111, *111
Willow Estate 5, 43, 60, 73
Willow Walk 16
Winchester Road 94
Winchmore Hill 12
Windmill 111, *111, *112
Windmill Hill station *86
Winters, Bernie 111
Wood Green 5
Woodlands Estate 43
Woodside Cottages 29
Woolpack Bridge 94
Worcester Lodge *46
Worcesters school 47, 99
Workhouses 7, 57, 84
Workmen's fares 87
Worlds End Lane 56, 111
Wright family 58
Wroth family 34, 111-112

YERKES, Charles Tyson 89